PAINT CAN!

techniques, patterns, and
projects for bringing
color into every room

SUNNY GOODE

photographs by KIP DAWKINS

Sterling Publishing Co., Inc.
New York

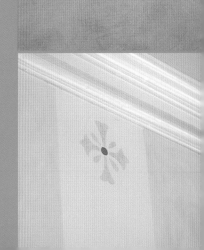

A Lark Production
3 West Main Street #103
Irvington, NY 10533

Library of Congress Cataloging-in-Publication Data

Goode, Sunny.
   Paint can! : techniques, patterns, and projects for bringing color into
every room / Sunny Goode.
      p. cm.
   Includes index.
   ISBN-13: 978-1-4027-3094-8
   ISBN-10: 1-4027-3094-2
   1. House painting--Amateurs' manuals. 2. Texture painting--Amateurs' manuals.
3. Interior decoration--Amateurs' manuals.   I. Title.
   TT323.G555 2006
   698'.14--dc22

                                    2006013720

10 9 8 7 6 5 4 3 2 1

Published by Sterling Publishing Co., Inc.

387 Park Avenue South, New York, NY 10016

©2006 by Sunny Goode

Distributed in Canada by Sterling Publishing

c/o Canadian Manda Group, 165 Dufferin Street

Toronto, Ontario, Canada M6K 3H6

Distributed in the United Kingdom by GMC Distribution Services

Castle Place, 166 High Street, Lewes, East Sussex, England BN7 1XU

Distributed in Australia by Capricorn Link (Australia) Pty. Ltd.

P.O. Box 704, Windsor, NSW 2756, Australia

Sterling ISBN-13: 978-4027-3094-8
        ISBN-10: 1-4027-3094-2

For information about custom editions, special sales, premium
and corporate purchases, please contact Sterling Special Sales
Department at 800-805-5489 or specialsales@sterlingpub.com.

acknowledgments

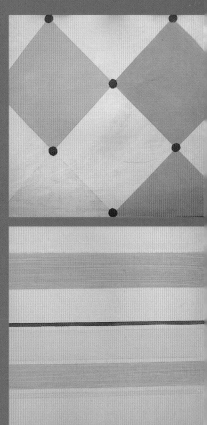

THIS BOOK IS DEDICATED to all who love to create! And also to my family, who have put up with my passion for paint my whole life: to Read, for supporting and living with an entrepreneurial experiment; to my kids, who keep me laughing; and to Isadore for her amazing patience. To Lucy, for always believing and for being there with humor; and to Martha, for not quitting. Thanks to Lisa DiMona, for seeing the potential for a book, calling, and making it happen! And to Kip Dawkins. That's hot. Thanks for your eye. At Sterling, my thanks to Julie Trelstad, for her vision, and to Isabel Stein, for attention to all the details.

A very, very special thanks to the following friends, who graciously shared their homes for photography throughout this book. I could not have produced this work without you all and I cannot put into words how much I appreciate it! Thank you for your support: The Ackerlys, Damgards, Fitzgeralds, Jordans, Kamaras, Gottwalds, Suellen Gregory, the Morgans, Rusbuldts, and Valentines. And special thanks to Nanny Baker and Ashley Quamme, who allowed me to learn from them, and to all of my clients, who have let me follow my passion for paint and have supported me throughout my career.

let the sun shine in

FOR AS LONG AS I CAN REMEMBER, I have been inspired by color. My parents always encouraged me to express myself artistically, but it was not until college, when I had the opportunity to study art in Italy, that I came to appreciate fully what color can do: the drama of a Titian red, the magic of fresco walls, the light in a Bellini. The styles and effects that inspired me as a student are part of the reason I became a decorative painter. And what a joy it was to discover that frescos and glazes can be replicated with modern-day paint.

I'm lucky that I've been able to indulge my personal passion for the decorative arts professionally, but I'm equally passionate about sharing the means for clients and customers to create beautifully painted walls, floors, ceilings, and furniture. I have long been a practitioner of custom decorative painting for individual clients and for myself. I've painted and repainted the rooms and surfaces in my own home so often that my husband never knows what to expect when he gets home from work! A few years ago I formed Sunny's Goodtime® Paints so that everyone could bring the look of old fresco plaster or stone walls or glazed finishes into their homes. This book is the next logical step in my mission to inspire and to teach anyone how to add decorative flourish with paint alone.

contents

"Paint is the **simple solution** to creating an environment that says what you want it to say and makes you feel the way you want to feel."

what paint can do

top: Panels break up the wall space in this living room. Brown and pink outlines enhance the yellow base color.

bottom: Express your personality and turn an inexpensive urn into something outstanding with shocking green high-gloss paint.

opposite: The architectural details of this built-in TV cabinet are highlighted with French blue-gray flat oil paint and aging glaze, mixed with raw umber.

COLOR EXPRESSES OUR PERSONALITY. The colors we wear or choose to put on our walls reflect who we are and affect our moods. Changing the color in a room can dramatically alter the context of the room and how we feel when we're in it: bright and cheery in a cool-palette breakfast nook or cozy and contemplative in a warm-hued library. Paint is the simple solution to creating an environment that says what you want it to say and makes you feel the way you want to feel. And the best part about paint, as one of my teachers used to say, is: *It is only paint!* You can always paint over it! She's right, of course. I was never afraid of painting anything, and I'm still surprised by people who are. I hope this book will unleash a bit of fearlessness in you. Paint. Paint. Paint. And paint. If the results are too dramatic or not dramatic enough, you can always paint again until you have what you want.

5

Pale blue stripes and thin brown pinstripes give a tailored look to this sitting room.

Color can do amazing things for our lives, especially the color we choose to surround ourselves with every day. Color can cheer us up, calm us down, or simply remind us that there is beauty in the world. Important as color is, your choice of color does not always have to be a big-deal, permanent statement. Many subtle changes can make a difference in your surroundings and your aesthetic satisfaction. In addition to overall eye appeal, paint—especially decorative paint—can achieve any of the following goals:

Highlight architectural details (or compensate for lack thereof). If you already have charming architectural details in your home, you will want to highlight them. If you lack such built-in gems, you can create the illusion with simple paint techniques. Consider adding a chair rail or paint panels; no one will guess they didn't come with the house.

Make a room look bigger. A classic trick for enlarging a room is to paint 12"-wide (30 cm) to 14"-wide (35 cm) vertical stripes. I usually suggest painting tone-on-tone colors (two different shades of the same color). This can form a subtle background for furnishings without stealing the spotlight. Another tip: To add height to a ceiling, paint it a light blue. You'll swear that it's a foot higher.

A painted canopy picks up the colors of the bedding in this bedroom. The border was planned in chalk and painted freehand. The dots were stenciled on. See page 114 for details.

The three-color rule is in evidence on these panels, painted in a warm yellow and outlined in a narrow line of pink and a wider line of brown.

Sunny's 3-color rule

Choose three basic colors for your home's interior, and then add accent colors room by room. For example, you might choose green, orange, and chocolate brown with accent colors of pink and aqua blue. The three-color rule makes it much easier to choose furnishings and accessories, and your home will feel more unified and pleasant when you are in it.

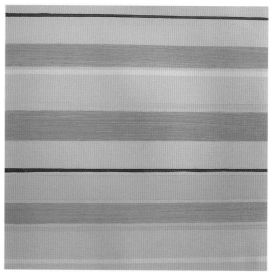

Horizontal stripes of varying widths in warm colors create a pleasant, modern look on this test board. The base color is a yellow-orange. Stripes of several widths were painted in brown, pink, green, and a very light tan.

To create harmony among the angles of this girl's room, we washed a darker green border of glaze (Sunny's Goodtime Gator Green Glaze) on the lower half of the green wall with a rag.

This kitchen cabinet took on a new personality when stripes of varying widths in three shades of orange were painted at the back.

Make a room look cozy. To make a room cozier, I almost always paint the ceiling the same color as the walls. The key, though, is to dilute the color formula for the ceiling to half-strength, which you can ask your paint supplier to do. This envelops the room in color and makes it feel more intimate. ("Half-strength" refers to paint mixed using one-half of the usual color formula per gallon.) Sometimes, if the walls are warm, I suggest a warm color for the ceiling as well, like a pale pink.

Make a room flatter you. It's always a good bet to use colors on the walls of your house that you tend to wear. Find colors that complement your individual coloring. It's your house, after all, so you should look the best in it!

Warm tones create a peaceful atmosphere and the three-color rule is at work in these panels, painted in a light yellow-orange and outlined in a narrow line of brown and a wider line of pink.

A children's room is transformed into a medieval castle by using the stoneblock technique on a base color of white.

Make a room seem soothing. Create a soothing room by using the same color on the walls and the ceiling and choosing one coordinating fabric for all the furniture. Take the color of the wall and use it half-strength on the ceiling. Keep your paint and fabric in the same color family; use all yellows, or pinks, or greens. Use different shades of the same color throughout the room, and instead of introducing too many colors, use fabrics that incorporate these shades.

Create harmony. Keep to the three-color rule to harmonize your entire home. Choose three colors, excluding the neutrals, and use different shades of those colors throughout your house in every room, even baths and closets.

Unify. When choosing trim color, use the same color throughout the entire house. This will unify the rooms and will also make touchups easier. When you are painting a room with dark or wood trim, choose a color for the walls and use the wall color formula half-strength for the ceiling. This will unify the room.

Green walls, panels washed in an aqua blue wash, and a coral border stenciled over in green give this wall a folk art feeling that harmonizes with the antiqued country-style decor.

Don't be afraid to try something daring, like these floor-to-ceiling diamonds. They add some fun, yet keep things simple. This is a nice idea for a child's room, a long hallway, or an office area. The subtle color difference is achieved by applying glaze with cheesecloth.

Make a statement with a message-board wall, done with chalkboard paint.

Make a statement. Don't be afraid to use a really intense color to make a bold statement where appropriate. Choose a sunflower yellow, hot pink, or lime green in high-gloss paint or in a texture like Venetian plaster for the entrance hall. It's fun to view from other rooms in the house, and you do not have to sit in it so long you may tire of it. You can do it. Even if you've never picked up a paint-brush, you will find that it's easy to paint. It's not all fun and games, of course. There are supplies to organize and surfaces to prepare. Other surfaces will need to be protected from paint. Sure, it's a little messy, and yes, there's the cleanup to deal with, but everything involved in a paint project gets you closer to where you want to be: swathed in luscious color. Almost as nice as the nearly instantaneous results you get with a do-it-yourself paint project is the satisfaction that you've done it all yourself.

tip

Paint panels above a chair rail to balance the furnishings in the room.

Multiple thin lines define these panels. The green and red lines tie in to the ceramics and other decorative elements in the room. The walls were first painted a light green, and then the panels were painted light cream.

paint 101

Once you know the basic paint facts outlined here, you're well on your way to a successful painting enterprise.

Paint Coats

PRIMER: The first coat applied to a surface. Primer helps paint adhere to what is being painted. Most projects in this book won't require primer; it's generally used on unpainted surfaces.

BASECOAT: Any layer of paint before the finish.

FINISH: The decorative, color-saturated paint applied after the basecoat. A second coat over the finish is usually optional, although more than one coat might be needed for certain colors, such as strong reds and pinks.

TOP COAT: The last layer of paint applied, which may be either the finish or a decorative coat over the finish.

Finishes can be classified as:

FLAT: A finish with no gloss.

MATTE/SATIN: A finish with minimal gloss.

EGGSHELL/PEARL: A finish with a little gloss.

SEMI-GLOSS/HIGH-GLOSS: Quite glossy/the glossiest possible finish.

Top coats include:

VARNISH: A clear top coat that determines the sheen on the wall.

GLAZE: A thin transparent coat, sometimes tinted, that goes over the finish to soften or enhance it. Glazes stay wet longer than colorwashes, and they can be manipulated with paint tools to create discernible patterns.

top: A fern green glaze and stencil over a pale green base color.

bottom: Apricot colorwash over a medium ivory base color.

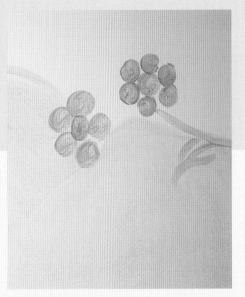

COLORWASH: A thin transparent coat, sometimes tinted, that goes over the finish to enhance it, creating a wash effect. It's like a glaze but thinner, and it is applied differently. A colorwash is more opaque than a glaze and is more highly pigmented. It covers more of the base color, dries quickly, and literally is made to be washed on the walls as if you were cleaning them with a rag. Some of the colorwashes used in this book are custom mixes. To get Sunny's Goodtime Avocado Colour Wash, for example, combine Sunny's Goodtime Gator Green Glaze with Sunny's Goodtime Lizard Lime Colour Wash in a clean mixing cup.

Freehand border and cantaloupe colorwash over a pale yellow base color.

CLEARCOAT: A colorless coat similar to a varnish that changes the sheen or protects a finish.

Other Paint Terms

LATEX PAINT: Latex paint is water-based, and you need only soap and water to clean it up.

OIL-BASED PAINT: Oil-based paint is just that, oil-based, and you'll need paint thinner to clean it up.

ENAMEL: A type of high-resin latex-based paint that is very durable and often glossy. There are also oil-based enamels.

BINDER: The part of the paint that holds the color together. Oil-based paints have an oil binder; latex-based paints have an acrylic binder.

DILUENT: The part of the paint that dilutes the binder and pigment until the paint is thin enough to be applied. A diluent compatible with oil is used in oil-based paints. Water is used as the diluent in latex-based paints, earning them their alternate name, "water-based paints."

Gray glaze over a light brown base color.

See the glossary on p.116 for other useful paint terms.

Note: Sunny's Goodtime® Paints, including glazes, colorwashes, and aging glazes, are available at select retailers as well as at www.sunnysgoodtimepaints.com. You may substitute other products to approximate those shown in this book, but color results may vary. See the swatch chart on page 123, and specific paint information on pages 118 to 122.

getting ready

Applying glaze at the start of colorwash.

SUPPLIES

STARTING A PAINTING PROJECT in your home is exciting, and you probably can't wait to see the final result, but organization is the key to enjoying a project and to getting the results you want. Gather all the basic supplies before you first dip a brush into the paint can, and you'll avoid a world of frustration. You'll also be able to show off your finished room a lot sooner. Make sure you have the items described below on hand before you start any painting project. (Additional supplies for specific projects are given in the project sections.)

+ **A box of clean rags or cotton T-shirts cut into good-sized pieces you can hold in the palm of your hand.** The rags should be light in color, preferably white. A newly dyed and/or unwashed colored T-shirt will bleed color onto your beautiful walls.

+ **Decorative painter's tape made by 3M.** This blue tape (called Scotch® Blue Painter's Tape) is light in tack but sticky enough to use when taping off trim in a room. It's

tip

Paint colors tend to be darker after they have dried on the walls. Sometimes I choose a color and then select one shade lighter as my actual paint color.

less likely to pull off the trim paint than a tackier tape. There are several brands of blue tape, but I've found this one works best—others peel paint off the walls. You can find it at hardware and paint stores.

* **A 2¹/₂" (6.5 cm) natural bristle brush.** Natural bristle brushes were especially created for use with oil paint, but I used one to paint all the glazes pictured in this book. The bristles are soft and make stippling pretty. To clean the brush after using latex-based paint, wash it with soap and water immediately after use and it will last a long time. You can find natural bristle brushes at paint and hardware stores. I prefer Wooster brand in the 2½" (6.5 cm) or 3" (7.5 cm) size.

* **Plastic level with a ruler on one side.** This handy device allows you to measure and create a level line at the same time. It can be found in hardware stores.

* **Colored chalk.** I use colored chalk to mark out everything from stripes to freehand patterns. It wipes off easily after the paint has dried and leaves virtually no sign it was

top: Testing a wash on a board.

bottom: Masking off a wall before painting a diamond.

17

getting ready

ever there. Select a chalk color in the same shade as your paint; for blue glaze, use blue chalk, and so on.

* **Brown paper tape.** This tape is light in tack and sticky on only one side. It is great for marking off and painting stripes, diamonds, plaids, panels, or any decorative painting pattern because it does not stick so much that it takes off the wallboard or plaster. You can find it at paint or hardware stores.

* **Fiberglass ladder, 4' (1.22 m) tall.** A lightweight and easy-to-maneuver ladder is key for painting. A shelf that can hold supplies is also a useful feature. You can reach most ceiling heights using a roller and pole with the 4' ladder, and it will fit nicely into almost any car. Fiberglass ladders are a little sturdier than aluminum ladders.

* **Roller, extension pole for roller, and roller tray.** Useful for reaching hard-to-get-at places and covering large areas smoothly and quickly.

* **Canvas drop cloth.** Invest in a 9' by 12' (2.7 m by 3.6 m) canvas drop cloth if you are going to do more than one painting project. I have three kids and keep a drop cloth in my car all the time; you would not believe how handy a drop cloth can be. A plastic tarp tends to get tangled up and does not lie flat, so canvas is a better choice.

* **Palette paper or wax paper.** For stenciling, I use a palette paper pad. This enables me to tap off excess glaze from my brush and mix color on the palette. Wax paper works just as well if you tape it over cardboard with some masking tape. Palette paper pads are available in art supply stores.

Masking off diamonds with decorative painter's tape and glazing.

- **Spackle.** A preparation must! Use to fill and conceal cracks, nail holes, and blemishes in plaster, wallboard, and wood. You can get it at the hardware store.

- **Sandpaper.** Use sandpaper to prepare trim or furniture. Depending on the project, use a fine- or coarse-grit paper, cut into a small square, and fold in half for more control.

- **Cleaning product.** I'm a huge fan of Mr. Clean Magic Eraser™ for tough spots. Natural cleansers such as soap and water work best for general cleaning.

- **Primer.** Use primer as a base layer to help paint adhere to the surface you are painting. Primer may also act as a stain killer and/or odor barrier.

- **Tape measure.** I use a small tape measure since it is lighter and easier to hold.

- **Sea sponge.** I use sea sponges for stencil projects. I like a small size that I can adjust easily with my fingertips so it will not spill over the stencil and onto the wall. I get the sponge wet first and then wring it out so it doesn't absorb too much paint and become heavy. Sea sponges can be found at hardware, art supply, and craft stores.

- **Bullet level.** I use a 9" (23 cm) level, which is great for hard-to-reach spaces over doors and windows. You can get it at the hardware store.

- **Artist's brush.** A size 8, 10, or 12 will get you through any decorative paint project in this book and most others as well.

- **Good attitude!** Guaranteed to make all your paint endeavors pleasant ones.

Floor paint and glaze let us transform
a wooden floor.

A large stencil adds whimsy to a formal room.

basics

CHOOSING PROJECTS
(or How to Use This Book)

Anyone can create artfully painted living spaces. Whether
you want to begin with something simple, such as a colorwash or a glaze, or whether you want to take on a more
complicated endeavor such as a diamond-patterned floor,
this book shows you everything you need to know. The
projects are organized loosely from basic to more advanced
techniques, but they are all easy enough if you follow the
step-by-step directions.

Perhaps the hardest part is deciding what you want to
paint first. If you do not yet know the kind of project you
want to undertake, flip through the book for ideas and
inspiration.

If you have never painted anything before, choose a
colorwash or glaze project first, as these are the easiest to
prepare and do. You may want to paint a single wall in a
room as an accent or focal point before you tackle a complete room. Or paint a ceiling half-strength of the wall
color just to get your feet wet (and see the lush results
such a color scheme provides).

Once you've done one project, you'll want to do more,
and you'll get more daring with every project you complete
successfully.

tip

Use a cotton ball dipped in nail-polish remover
to determine whether the paint on your existing
walls is latex-based or oil-based. Rub the cotton
ball on the wall. If the paint becomes shiny, it is
oil-based; if it becomes gooey and comes off
onto the cotton ball, it is latex.

tip

Be sure to let a latex basecoat dry for at least a week before applying a glaze or wash over it. Dry to the touch does not mean the paint has cured. If it has not cured, the glazes or washes will re-wet the paint.

PREPARATION

In general, changing a room with paint is relatively easy, but preparation is the ultimate key to success. First consider the existing condition of the walls you plan to paint. If the walls have been painted recently and are in great condition, you are ready to go. If the existing paint is peeling or if it is dusty or scuffed, you have some prep work to do before you start to paint. Glazes and colorwashes are transparent, and any stains or marks that are already on your walls will show through them especially. Take care to prep walls and surfaces thoroughly.

1 Vacuum or dust all surfaces.

2 Scrub scuffs and wall marks with water or a specialty product; I love Mr. Clean Magic Eraser, which works like a dream on flat wall surfaces.

3 Scrape off peeling paint or loose plaster, and then fill in with spackle. Smooth and let dry. Once the areas are dry, sand lightly.

4 Prime all areas that have been filled with spackle and sanded. If you are going to use a latex paint, walls that are already painted with oil-based paint need to be primed as well. A shellac or alcohol-based primer will help the paint adhere to the surface. Many primers also act as stain killers and/or odor barriers.

5 Use a latex eggshell base paint in your chosen color as your basic paint. Once this is dry, you're ready for the fun that is decorative painting!

A palm stencil in white latex was sponged over a base color of blue-gray. An irregular dot stencil in gold was added.

A warm glaze over gray enlivens a pool house.

"What a joy it was to discover that frescoes and glazes can be replicated with modern-day paint!"

part 2 techniques

you can do it!

To add balance to the window treatment, we drew attention to the green walls by adding a deeper green glaze. The base color is light olive green (Benjamin Moore latex eggshell 391). The colorwash is Sunny's Goodtime Avocado Colour Wash combination color (12 oz. Gator Green Glaze + 12 oz. Lizard Lime Colour Wash).

colorwash

what you need:

- **Basecoat: Light olive green paint (Benjamin Moore latex eggshell 391)**
- **Sunny's Goodtime Avocado Colour Wash combination color (12 oz. Gator Green Glaze + 12 oz. Lizard Lime Colour Wash)**
- **2 ½" (6.5 cm) natural bristle brush**
- **1" (2.5 cm) blue painter's tape for trim**
- **White cotton T-shirt or rag**
- **Drop cloth**
- **Ladder**

COLORWASHING ADDS layers of translucent color to your wall. It's a quick and easy technique that creates a soft, watercolor-like effect. I like to use the same family of colors for colorwashing; warms (yellows, oranges, pinks, and reds) or cools (blues, greens, and purples) always go together. Try colorwashing a piece of furniture for a weathered, distressed look. You instantly get the effect some paints achieve only after being exposed to the elements for years and years.

Colorwashed walls recall the appearance of fresco plaster or faded cotton. Colorwashing your walls does not require fancy techniques or the manipulation of paint products with special tools. Instead, colorwash is meant to be applied with a rag, as if you were literally washing or cleaning the walls.

Colorwash covers more of the base paint than a glaze does, leaving a casual finish that does not carry a sheen. For sheen and extra depth, you may want to add a glaze on top of a colorwash, but the examples you see here are simply colorwashed for glorious effects.

Colorwash done on a medium ivory base color. Sunny's Goodtime Apricot Colour Wash was washed on with a rag.

Prior to starting to colorwash, basecoat the walls (in our model, light olive green paint was used). Let dry for a week.

INSTRUCTIONS FOR COLORWASH

1 Using the brush, apply a large X of the avocado colorwash on the wall, about 10" (25 cm) across (Photo 1).

2 As though you're washing a window, use a rag to rub in the X, "washing" evenly to prevent dark lines of colorwash from forming at the edges of your ragging (Photo 2).

3 Apply more colorwash X's and rub in the paint in random patterns. Think jigsaw puzzle, and avoid consistent up and down or side to side application, which could result in a noticeable pattern (Photo 3).

4 Take excess paint off the brush with the rag and stipple carefully into the corners with the brush. The finished room can be seen on page 24.

tips

* Colorwash looks best when washed over a latex eggshell-finish basecoat.

* Colorwash will darken as it dries, so apply it lightly.

* Colorwash on a practice board first. I've been known to test colorwash or any technique or pattern on shirtboards from the dry cleaner.

* Don't change rags in the middle of a wall. The rag absorbs so much product that you'll get variations in color depth. If you need to stop in the middle of a project, store your rag sealed in a plastic zippered food bag. This way you can pick up where you left off.

Photo 1. Apply a colorwash X about 10" (25 cm) across.

Photo 2. Rub the colorwash evenly with a rag, as though washing a window.

Photo 3. Apply more colorwash, and rub it around in random patterns.

To cozy up this large living room, we washed the walls with a beautiful light orange. The base color was a pale yellow. Sunny's Goodtime Buttercup Baby Colour Wash (12 oz.) was mixed with Sunny's Goodtime Apricot Colour Wash (8 oz.) for the colorwash.

more colorwash

top: To create harmony among the angled walls of this girl's bedroom, we washed a darker green border on the lower half of the wall. The scalloped border mimics an architectural element and is a nice backdrop for the furniture. Colorwashing a deep border is less time-consuming than doing an entire wall; your work is cut in half. Sunny's Goodtime Gator Green Glaze was washed on with a rag.

bottom: The ceiling height in this pool house presented a color challenge, and we also wanted to tie in with the natural wood tones from the stained beadboard ceiling. We used two techniques to get depth and texture. First we washed the walls with a muted gray and then we used a warm glaze to connect to the wood from the ceiling. The paint techniques go nicely with the handmade light fixtures the customer found in the islands. The wash is Sunny's Goodtime French Gray Colour Wash, and the glaze is Sunny's Goodtime Take Me to Tuscany, a warm, reddish brown.

To warm up this large dining room, we painted the ceiling a very pale pink and the trim a creamy white. The soft, sophisticated look of the walls is achieved by colorwashing pink (Sunny's Goodtime Palm Beach Pink Colour Wash) over a light taupe base.

Here the base color is taupe, Benjamin Moore latex eggshell 976. Sunny's Goodtime Cantaloupe Glaze combination color (12 oz. Pumpkin Glaze + 12 oz. Sunshine Daydream Glaze) was washed on with a rag. The custom stencil was done in Sunny's Goodtime Bubblegum Pink Colour Wash (16 oz. Palm Beach Pink Colour Wash + 8 oz. Ruby Red Glaze.

stencil

what you need:

- **Basecoat: Taupe paint (Benjamin Moore latex eggshell 976)**
- **Sunny's Goodtime Canteloupe Glaze combination color (12 oz. Pumpkin Glaze + 12 oz. Sunshine Daydream Glaze)**
- **Sunny's Goodtime Bubblegum Pink Colour Wash combination color (16 oz. Palm Beach Pink Colour Wash + 8 oz. Ruby Red Glaze)**
- **Sea sponge**
- **Palette paper, wax paper, or a paper plate**
- **Stencil**
- **Blue painter's tape**

STENCILING IS AS SIMPLE as it sounds: blotting paint from a sponge or brush onto a cutout of any shape. The result is a pattern with a charmingly handmade look.

Stencils are versatile enough to use any number of ways, and since you choose the shape yourself, a stencil makes a personal statement on walls, ceilings, floors, or furniture. Stencils can be sophisticated or whimsical. They are eye-catching, and their effect is original on any wall. Use over-sized stencils either at the bottom or the top of a color-washed wall to add pattern and character to an expanse of wall. Spice up classic patterns by using a small stencil to accent alternating stripes or diamond intersections.

When choosing stencil patterns, keep in mind the scale and the effect that you are trying to achieve.

The base color is a light blue-gray. Sunny's Goodtime French Blue/Gray Glaze combination color (10 oz. Marine + 14 oz. Ocean Age Aging Glaze) was washed on the wall with a rag. Sunny's Goodtime Palm Stencil was sponged with white latex paint. Sunny's Goodtime Irregular Dot Stencil was sponged with Sunny's Goodtime Metallic Gold Stencil Paint.

I like small metallic stencils on ceilings and larger stencils for walls. If you want a big impact, use a large-scale stencil in vibrant colors and keep the rest of the room more neutral.

Prior to starting to stencil, basecoat the walls (in our model, taupe paint was used). Let dry for a week.

INSTRUCTIONS FOR STENCILING

The basics for stenciling apply to all the projects you see in the following pages:

1 Tape the stencil on with blue painter's tape to keep it in place (Photo 1).

2 Lightly dip your sponge into the cantelope glaze and then tap directly on top of the stencil (Photos 2 and 3). I tend to tap in a triangular pattern; this dappling or stippling technique gives the stenciled patterns a hand-made look.

3 For this particular pattern, I spaced the stencils about 2" (5 cm) apart. For smaller stencils, a good rule of thumb is to space stencils from fingertip to elbow or about 12" apart.

4 Remove the stencil (Photo 4) and repeat until you have finished the entire room (see photo on page 30).

Photo 1. Tape the stencil onto the wall.

Photo 2. Tap the glaze onto the stencil with the sponge.

Photo 3. Keep tapping the glaze on.

Photo 4. When you have finished a section, carefully remove the stencil.

tip

Make your own stencil. I had my hand-drawn design enlarged at the copy store and then laminated. I cut out the pattern with an X-acto knife to create the stencil.

Voila! The glazed and stenciled wall.

more stencils

above left and right: I hand-cut this 20" by 20" (50 by 50 cm) damask pattern stencil to make a bold statement. Note that the stencil is positioned right side up, then upside down, and then right side up again for added interest. The stencils are spaced 22" (55 cm) apart. The base color is a light pink. Sunny's Goodtime Rosey Rosey Glaze was washed on with a rag. The custom-made stencil was also done in Rosey Rosey Glaze, showing how the same paint can result in two different effects when different application techniques are used. Sunny's Goodtime Original Aging Glaze was washed on top.

opposite, bottom: Stenciling looks great in just about any color and works for traditional, formal rooms as well as more contemporary ones. This large-scale stencil adds whimsy to a formal and somewhat traditional room. The pattern is used above and below the chair rail for greater uniformity and impact. Had there been wainscoting beneath the chair rail—a detail common to rooms with chair rails—I would have painted the wainscoting the same color as the walls to add weight to the lower wall. Gray is always a good bet when you are choosing a base color to stencil on. An aging glaze was applied with a rag on top of the stenciling in this room. The base color is light gray. The custom-made stencil was done in Sunny's Goodtime Bubblegum Pink Glaze combination color (16 oz. Palm Beach Pink + 8 oz. Ruby Red). The entire wall was aged in Sunny's Goodtime Original Aging Glaze, a brownish glaze, washed on with a rag.

top: This vertical stencil adorns a bathroom wall that was glazed with a rag in fern green over the basecoat of pale green. The glaze adds patina to a newly constructed wall. Using a level/ruler, mark vertical lines with chalk and then stencil on top of the lines. Sunny's Goodtime Fern Glaze combination color (4 oz. Original Aging Glaze + 20 oz. Gator Green Glaze) was washed on with a rag. Then Sunny's Goodtime Original Aging Glaze was sponged onto a custom-made stencil.

I added texture to the walls in this hallway by painting a yellow glaze on top of a yellow base. Now these walls tie in to the green glazed walls in the adjoining family room (see p. 24). The basecoat is a medium yellow (Farrow & Ball latex eggshell 218), and Sunny's Goodtime Summer Sun Glaze combination color (20 oz. Sunshine Daydream Glaze + 4 oz. Original Aging Glaze) was ragged on top.

glaze

what you need:

- ◆ **Basecoat: Medium yellow paint (Farrow & Ball latex eggshell 218)**
- ◆ **Sunny's Goodtime Summer Sun Glaze combination color (20 oz. Sunshine Daydream Glaze + 4 oz. Original Aging Glaze)**
- ◆ **2 ½" (6.5 cm) natural bristle brush**
- ◆ **1" (2.5 cm) blue painter's tape for trim**
- ◆ **White cotton T-shirt or rag**
- ◆ **Drop cloth**
- ◆ **Ladder**

GLAZE IS A SHEER transparent color that adds richness and depth to a normally flat color. If the effect of colorwash is to give walls the kind of variation and light you see in faded cotton or fresco plaster, then glazing creates a look like silk. Imagine two pieces of fabric that are the same color, but one is cotton and the other is silk. The cotton fabric is a consistently flat color, but silk holds a range of colors and shimmers in different lights. The depth and variation in shading you see in silk is the effect you get when you glaze an existing wall. It may look like the work of a professional when you're done, but the process is easy.

Glaze has a higher pigment content than colorwash, but at the same time it is more transparent. You see more of the basecoat through the glaze. It also has a pretty sheen. You can use different tools to manipulate and apply glaze, since the product stays wet long enough to hold the pattern of whatever tool you are using.

On the test board shown, the base color is a light brown. Sunny's Goodtime Black Leather Glaze was applied with a rag.

Use a crumpled-up rag to achieve a leathery glaze. For a softer, more subtle look, use cheesecloth. Glaze applied on top of bold colors works beautifully to soften and lend dimension to the walls. The textured appearance of glazed walls works best in rooms that are more formal.

Prior to glazing, basecoat the walls (in our model, medium yellow paint was used). Let dry for a week.

INSTRUCTIONS FOR GLAZING

1 Tape off all the trim with the blue tape (Photo 1).

2 Dip the brush into the glaze (Photo 2).

3 Apply a large X of glaze onto the wall (Photo 3).

4 Take a rag or cheesecloth and pat around the X evenly while rotating your wrists to get the desired richness. Make sure all edges pat out evenly. Glaze stays wet longer than colorwash, so lightly tap your rag or cheesecloth and keep looking at what you are doing, not for pattern but for color depth. Try not to be heavy-handed in some areas and light-handed in others, unless this differentiation is the effect you want (Photo 4). Keep moving in an irregular direction, avoiding consistent up and down or side to side motions that yield a discernible pattern. Think jigsaw puzzle.

5 Take excess paint off the brush with the rag (Photo 5) and then stipple into the corners and edges with the brush (Photo 6). The finished room can be seen on page 36.

Photo 1. First tape the trim to protect it.

Photo 2. Dip the brush in the glaze.

Photo 3. Apply an X of glaze to the wall.

Photo 4. Apply the glaze with a rag

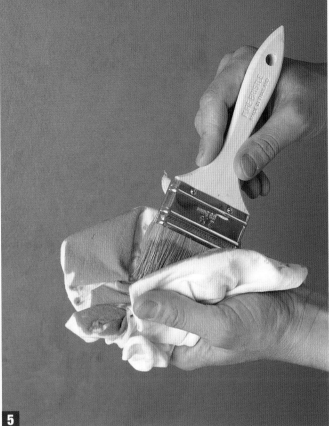

Photo 5. Remove the excess paint from the brush.

tips

* Glaze may be applied with a cotton rag, as for colorwash, but you can also achieve great results with cheesecloth, a plastic bag, or a sea sponge. To find the texture that appeals to you most, test the glaze application with various materials on a board.

* Walls covered with latex paint can be the base for either a latex or an oil glaze, but walls covered with oil-based paints can only receive an oil-based glaze.

Photo 6. Stipple the edges and corners with the brush.

more glazes

The glaze on this sitting room wall adds subtle texture and makes the resulting pink wall color sophisticated rather than juvenile. These walls, in combination with the painted floor, are warm enough to ground the room without overpowering it. The base color is white. Old Masters Tinting Glaze, tinted with artist's tube oil in alizarin crimson, was rolled on and then tapped with a cheesecloth.

Glazing adds warmth and also balances the heavier furniture typically found in a family den. The base color is a light tan. Sunny's Goodtime Original Aging Glaze was applied with a rag.

The glaze makes a lighter color work in this timeless dining room. We pulled a yellow green from the rug to keep the room light, but we also wanted the color to be strong. The ceilings are high and the moldings grand so the glazed walls add just enough weight to balance the room. The base color is white. Sunny's Goodtime Fern Glaze combination color (4 oz. Original Aging Glaze + 20 oz. Gator Green Glaze) was applied on with a cheesecloth.

The wall and trim are painted the same color here because the room has very little wall space. A glaze rubbed on with a rag adds interest and is counterbalanced by an airy blue ceiling. The base color is a light tan. Sunny's Goodtime Original Aging Glaze was washed on top.

The walls and trim are painted the same base color to unify the room. A tonal glaze adds interest and depth. The treatment is classic and simple. The base color is beige. Sunny's Goodtime Original Aging Glaze was ragged on top.

My entry hall is Venetian plaster tinted with hot pink. (I love the texture of Venetian plaster even though it will be quite a job to remove if I ever decide I want a change.) The hot pink makes for pleasant viewing from the adjoining rooms and is very livable in an entry hall, where it is not overpowering. The Venetian plaster is a Behr product, custom-mixed.

above and opposite: Here the base color is taupe, Benjamin Moore latex eggshell 976. Sunny's Goodtime Cantaloupe Glaze combination color (12 oz. Pumpkin + 12 oz. Sunshine Daydream) was washed on with a rag. The custom-made stencil was done in Sunny's Goodtime Bubblegum Pink Glaze.

aging glaze

what you need:

- **Basecoat: Taupe paint for the baseboard (Benjamin Moore latex flat 976)**
- **Sunny's Goodtime Original Aging Glaze**
- **Top coat: Clear polyacrylic or polyurethane**
- **Sandpaper**
- **Shellac or alcohol-based primer**
- **2 ½" (6.5 cm) natural bristle brush**
- **White cotton T-shirt or rag**
- **Brown paper tape for the top of the baseboard**
- **1" (2.5 cm) blue painter's tape for the bottom of the baseboard**

AGING GLAZES CAN GIVE an heirloom quality to a chair you pick up at the mall or a time-honored look to a newly constructed home. In fact, it's easier to get a new "old" look with aging glaze than with a complete overhaul: just pick up a rag and get to it.

It's possible to give character to a new wall trim or piece of furniture using latex aging glazes, gel stains, or tube oil paints mixed with clear oil glaze. In our demonstration, a baseboard was aged.

A piece of furniture with good lines always lends itself to an aging glaze. If your furniture is already painted with oil paint, you must use an oil-based glaze. Apply a polyacrylic or polyurethane top coat to glazed furniture for added protection.

Aging glaze works wonders on baseboards and woodwork.

PREPARING THE SURFACE FOR AGING GLAZE

1 Sand the baseboard or other area to a smooth finish.

2 Prime with a shellac or alcohol-based primer, which will help paint adhere to the surface. After the primer has dried, paint the surface with the latex basecoat (taupe in our model).

APPLYING THE AGING GLAZE TO THE BASEBOARD

1 Protect the walls with the brown tape and the floor with the blue tape (Photo 1).

2 Brush on the glaze (Photo 2) and rub it in with a rag as if you were washing your windows (Photo 3).

3 Apply more glaze by dabbing with the brush, rather than rubbing with the rag, to create an even older appearance (Photo 4).

4 Remove the tape (Photo 5).

5 Allow the glaze to dry.

6 Finish up with a polyacrylic or polyurethane top coat for added durability. The completed room can be seen on page 46.

Photo 1. Protect the walls and floor with tape.

Photo 2. Brush the glaze onto the baseboard.

Photo 3. Rub the glaze in with a rag.

Photo 4. Dab on more glaze with the brush for patina and depth.

Photo 5. Remove the tape.

tip

If your furniture is already painted with oil paint, you must use an oil glaze. Mix any clear oil glaze with raw umber artist's tube oil paint. Squeeze 3" (7.5 cm) of raw umber artist's tube oil paint into 1 quart (.94 L) of clear glaze, and mix thoroughly. This will create a lot of aging glaze, so divide these quantities according to the amount you need. Raw umber pigment is strong, and a little bit goes a long way.

more aging glazes

This chair was painted, sanded, and rubbed with an aging glaze. It was then gilded with gold leaf, rather than gold paint. I painted the lattice pattern on the caning. The multiple steps involved are well worth the effort. See Tip on page 49 for more on oil glaze. The base color is a warm light gray, and the highlights are a slightly darker warm gray. The entire chair was aged with Old Masters Tinting Glaze mixed with artist's tube oil in raw umber.

left: Once glazed, this 1950s French reproduction chair is at home with more authentic older pieces. The chair was first painted in light tan and then aged with Old Masters Tinting Glaze mixed with artist's tube oil in raw umber.

To give this mammoth built-in TV cabinet some personality, we painted the exterior, including the crown molding, a French blue-gray oil flat paint. We glazed the cabinet and then painted the interior a deep chocolate brown. This new piece is now imbued with some history. What a transformation! The entire cabinet was aged with Old Masters Tinting Glaze mixed with artist's tube oil in raw umber.

If you want color but also calm, paint the walls full strength with your chosen color and paint the ceiling the same color, but only half-strength. Age the furnishings, and you have plenty of color, but the less color-saturated ceiling calms things down. This is my bedroom, and I love all the variations of the same color. I even found readymade curtains that matched. The furniture is also painted in the same family of blue. The base color of the walls is a light blue-gray. The furniture was painted in light blue-gray and aged with Sunny's Goodtime Original Aging Glaze.

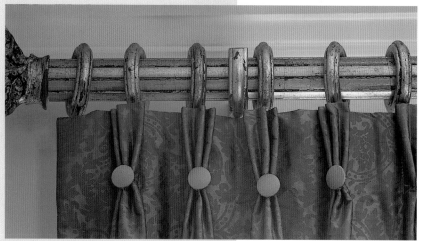

Gilded curtain rods add glamour to any room or window treatment. As projects go, this one is easy and provides nearly instant gratification. The rod looks like you might have found it at an estate sale. The poles and finials were painted in a reddish brown and then gilded with gold leaf.

My best advice when painting a chair or small table is to place it on a table so you are not sitting on the floor when you work.

This cabinet has been brought to life with gold highlights and glaze. Exemplifying what I mean by "good lines" in a piece of furniture, the three drawers balance the top doors, which are paneled with chicken wire. A simple gold trim enhances the lines, and an aging glaze lends elegance and authority. The cabinet was painted in a light gray latex flat. The highlights were done in Sunny's Goodtime Metallic Gold Stencil Paint. The entire piece was aged with Sunny's Goodtime Original Aging Glaze.

I found a pair of demi-lune tables at an antiques store, but they were not antiques. I had no idea how I was going to paint them, or where they would go, but I knew they would be great somewhere. Now they are chocolate brown with a bit of gilding and work nicely in my living room. The tables were painted in brown latex flat. Sunny's Goodtime Black Leather Glaze was rubbed on top, and the tables were gilded with gold leaf.

above and opposite: White and green colorwashed stripes give a clean, crisp look to this sitting room. The wide wall stripe is an interesting counterbalance to the narrow stripes in the rug, and the effect is bold and striking. The base color is Benjamin Moore latex eggshell Decorators White. The 14"-wide (35 cm) green stripes were washed on in Sunny's Goodtime Avocado Colour Wash combination color (12 oz. Lizard Lime Colour Wash + 12 oz. Gator Green Glaze).

vertical stripes

what you need:

- ♦ **Basecoat: White paint (Benjamin Moore latex eggshell Decorators White in model)**
- ♦ **Green colorwash: Sunny's Goodtime Avocado Colour Wash in model (12 oz. Lizard Lime Colour Wash + 12 oz. Gator Green Glaze)**
- ♦ **Tape measure**
- ♦ **24" (61 cm) plastic level with ruler; a 9" (23 cm) one for measuring above and below windows is also helpful**
- ♦ **2" (5 cm) brown paper tape**
- ♦ **1" (2.5 cm) blue painter's tape for trim**
- ♦ **Chalk**
- ♦ **2 ½" (6.5 cm) natural bristle brush**
- ♦ **Drop cloth**
- ♦ **Ladder**

VERTICAL STRIPING, or "lining," is a classic decorative pattern that's always in style. Stripes can enliven any room, whether the stripes are tone-on-tone, multicolored, of varying widths, uniform, laid on with precision, or painted to look more handmade.

Irregularly shaped rooms can be pulled together with simple stripes. Long, rectangular rooms can be foreshortened with stripes. Small spaces can be made jaunty with different-colored stripes. Stripes are so versatile they can be used for a living room, dining room, kitchen, bathroom, or child's room.

Vertical stripes can unify any room of the house. They elevate the ceiling and open up the room. If you colorwash or glaze the stripes with a color that is one shade deeper than the base color, you will create a room with long-lasting appeal. Once you get the measuring, taping, and chalking done, the technique is as simple as coloring in the lines.

1

2

3

Prior to painting stripes, basecoat the walls (in our model, white paint was used). Let dry for a week.

MARKING OFF FOR VERTICAL STRIPES

1 Begin in one corner of the room.

2 Measure 12" (30 cm) along the wall from the corner and mark with chalk (Photo 1).

3 Continue around the room, measuring 12" (30.5 cm) between chalk marks.

4 If the last stripe is too wide or too narrow, offset the irregular width by combining the width of the last two stripes and dividing that width in half, using one-half for each stripe. Once the room is complete, you won't notice the off-size width.

5 Use a level to mark vertical lines with chalk at the 12" (30.5 cm) marks from ceiling to floor (Photo 2).

6 If a painted stripe will butt up to another painted stripe at the corner of the room, or if an unpainted stripe will butt up to another unpainted stripe, halve the width of one stripe so it becomes 2 stripes at the corner. In effect, you are adding one more stripe.

7 Tape off the baseboard trim to protect it, using blue painter's tape.

8 Lay out a drop cloth under the first wall you plan to paint.

9 Tape off the edges of one stripe at a time as you paint, using brown paper tape (Photo 3).

Photo 1. Mark 12" (30 cm) intervals for vertical stripes in chalk.

Photo 2. Mark vertical lines with chalk, using a level.

Photo 3. Tape off edges of stripes with brown paper tape.

Photo 4. Brush on the colorwash and rub with a rag.

Photo 5. Remove brown tape after painting one stripe.

PAINTING THE VERTICAL STRIPES

1 Brush on the avocado colorwash in the middle of the stripe (at the top) and then rub it around with a rag, as if you were washing a window. If you begin in the middle of the stripe and work out to the edges of the tape, paint will not bleed under the tape (Photo 4).

2 Colorwash in this manner from the top of the stripe down to the bottom.

3 Remove any excess colorwash from the brush with the rag, and then use the brush to stipple the top and bottom edges to achieve a smooth, professional finish.

4 After one stripe has been colorwashed, remove the brown tape and move on to the next stripe (Photo 5).

5 Pull the blue tape off the trim after one whole wall is complete. Pulling tape off is fun, and revealing your neat handiwork gives you a great sense of accomplishment.

6 Finish each wall in the same manner. The finished room can be seen on page 54.

tips

* A 12"-wide (30.5 cm) stripe is recommended for most rooms. Never go less than 8" (20 cm) wide. The wider the stripe, the bigger the room will appear.

* Use blue tape for protecting the trim, and use brown paper tape for your walls. The brown paper tape is less tacky and will not remove your basecoat.

57

vertical stripes

more vertical stripes

Tonal stripes distinguish the walls of this entrance hall. The basecoat is light green; the stripes are Sunny's Goodtime Gator Green Glaze.

Create even more interest by adding a stencil to alternating stripes, using the same color or color family in the stencil. The base color is a pale yellow. The 12"-wide (30.5 cm) stripes were washed on in Sunny's Goodtime Summer Sun Glaze combination color (4 oz. Original Aging Glaze + 20 oz. Sunshine Daydream Glaze). The custom-made stencil and darker stripe were done in Sunny's Summer Sun Glaze. Sunny's Goodtime Dot Stencil was done in Sunny's Metallic Gold Stencil Paint.

A pinstripe detail gives this sitting room a smart, tailored look. Once the walls are striped, a glaze adds depth and finish. The base color is white. The 12"-wide (30.5 cm) stripes were done in gray-blue mixed with Sunny's Goodtime Clear Glaze, and the ¼"-wide (6 mm) stripes were done in a medium brown. The whole wall was washed with Sunny's Goodtime Cappuccino Glaze.

Painting stripes at the back of a cabinet adds color without your having to stripe an entire room. Stripes of varying widths were painted in three shades of orange latex flat on a white basecoat.

These stripes are so understated that you hardly notice them at first, but they give the room structure. This treatment works with any color palette, especially in lighter shades. The base color is white. The 12"-wide (30.5 cm) stripes were done in white mixed with Sunny's Goodtime Clear Glaze.

above left and right: Give an old dresser a facelift with simple stripes. This dresser was painted white, striped with pink and red, and then sanded and aged; when it gets beat up, you won't even notice! A piece like this can be used in any room that needs a dramatic color accent. Handsome knobs complete the picture. The base color is an oil semi-gloss white. The pink and red stripes were done in enamel. The entire piece was first lightly sanded and then aged with Old Masters Tinting Glaze mixed with raw umber artist's tube oil.

This cornice was rescued from a junk pile. The stripes add zip to the room, and the tractor in the center gives a focal point. The cornice board base color is latex eggshell white. The stripes and tractor were hand-painted in various artist's tube paints.

Horizontal stripes are an elegant surprise in this bathroom. The base color is pale blue-gray, Benjamin Moore latex flat HC-150. The 12"-wide (30.5 cm) horizontal stripes were painted in medium chocolate brown, Benjamin Moore latex flat 992.

horizontal stripes

what you need:

- ◆ **Basecoat: Pale blue-gray paint (Benjamin Moore latex flat HC-150)**
- ◆ **Stripes: Medium chocolate brown paint (Benjamin Moore latex flat 992)**
- ◆ **Chalk**
- ◆ **Level/ruler**
- ◆ **2 ½" (6.5 cm) natural bristle brush**
- ◆ **2" (5 cm) brown paper tape**
- ◆ **Ladder**
- ◆ **Drop cloth**

HORIZONTAL STRIPES give unexpected verve and a pleasant, modern look to any room. Hallways can be accentuated or made to appear longer, and small rooms can be made to appear more spacious with horizontal stripes. Bold bands of color are refreshing and can be used in any style of interior. Paint horizontal stripes on the longest wall in a small living room to make the room feel bigger. Use broad horizontal stripes to open up a tiny bathroom or add architectural interest in a bedroom.

Horizontal stripes of varying widths in warm colors create a pleasant, modern look. The base color is a yellow-orange. Stripes of several widths were painted in brown, pink, green, and a very light tan.

INSTRUCTIONS FOR HORIZONTAL STRIPES

Here a bold horizontal stripe is achieved with paint rather than with a glaze. The walls and ceiling are painted in the same pale blue-gray basecoat to start. The 12"-wide (30.5 cm) chocolate brown stripes pop against the white tile and floor.

MARKING OFF FOR HORIZONTAL STRIPES

1 Measure 12" (30.5 cm) up from the floor with a level/ruler and mark with chalk.

2 Continue marking 12" (30.5 cm) spans up the wall until you reach the ceiling (Photo 1).

3 Use the level to chalk a horizontal line around the room at the height of each mark (Photo 2).

4 Tape off the stripe that you intend to paint by applying the tape so that the lower edge of the top tape is against the upper line of the stripe area to be painted and the upper edge of the bottom tape is against the lower line of your stripe area (Photos 3 and 4).

5 Continue marking off and taping stripes around the room.

Photo 1. Measure up from the floor with a level/ruler.

Photo 2. Chalk a horizontal line around the room.

Photo 3. Define the upper limit of the stripe with brown tape above the chalk mark.

Photo 4. Define the lower limit of the stripe with brown tape below the chalk mark (upper edge of tape aligns with chalk mark).

Photo 5. Paint inside the taped edges.

PAINTING THE HORIZONTAL STRIPES

1 Once a stripe is completely taped, paint or glaze inside the taped edges (Photo 5). For this particular project, we painted our stripes with a flat paint, but glazing or colorwashing works just as well.

2 When the paint is dry, remove the tape (Photo 6). Voila! The finished bathroom can be seen on page 62.

Photo 6. Remove the tape.

more horizontal stripes

above and opposite: The walls in this boy's room are painted a warm tan, with darker stripes done in glaze. The nice thing about this design is that he won't outgrow it. The 12"-wide (30.5 cm) horizontal stripes were washed on in Sunny's Goodtime Original Aging Glaze.

tips

* Place a small piece of brown tape on the stripes that are not being painted so you remember to skip over them and know which stripes to paint.

* Use stripes to unify a room, even one with an awkward corner like the room on page 67.

horizontal stripes

Tone-on-tone plaid. The base color is pale yellow, Benjamin Moore latex eggshell 338. The plaid was done in Sunny's Goodtime Summer Sun Glaze combination color (20 oz. Sunshine Daydream mixed with 4 oz. Original Aging Glaze).

plaid

what you need:

- ◆ **Basecoat: Pale yellow paint (Benjamin Moore latex eggshell 338)**
- ◆ **Plaid lines: Sunny's Goodtime Summer Sun Glaze combination color (20 oz. Sunshine Daydream Glaze + 4 oz. Original Aging Glaze) in model**
- ◆ **2½" (6.5 cm) natural bristle brush**
- ◆ **24" (61 cm) plastic level with ruler**
- ◆ **2" (5 cm) brown paper tape**
- ◆ **1" (2.5 cm) blue painter's tape for trim**
- ◆ **Chalk**
- ◆ **Drop cloth**
- ◆ **Ladder**

P

PLAID BRINGS WOVEN fabric to mind and adds both coziness and color to your room. It's a simple combination of vertical and horizontal stripes, often done with glaze. Tone-on-tone plaids recall the gingham of summertime. You might not want to paint an entire room in plaid, especially if the room is small, but for a space that might never be the center of attention otherwise, plaid makes a statement and adds charm. Use plaid on a focal-point wall.

Prior to starting the plaid, basecoat the room (in our model, pale yellow paint was used). Let dry for a week.

It's easy to paint plaid, but it takes two days: one day to paint the vertical stripes, 24 hours of drying time, and one day to paint the horizontal stripes.

Tone-on-tone plaid in earth tones on a sample board. The base color is a dark green. The varying-width stripes were painted in beige, pale blue, and pale green. The entire design was aged with Sunny's Original Aging Glaze.

1

2

3

INSTRUCTIONS FOR PLAID, DAY 1

The plaid is made up of wide vertical and horizontal stripes.

Marking the Vertical Stripes

1 Measure 8" (20 cm) from the corner, and mark the wall with chalk.

2 Continue marking the wall, measuring 8" (20 cm) between each mark (Photo 1). Because the wall space here is in a small dormer, we used 8" (20 cm) stripes. To replicate the same idea on a larger wall, mark off 12" (30.5 cm) stripes.

3 If the last stripe is too wide or too narrow, offset the irregular width by combining the width of the last stripe and the stripe beside it, dividing that total in half, and using one-half for each stripe. Once the room is complete, you won't notice the off-size width.

4 Using the level, draw the vertical lines with chalk all along the wall, at the chalk marks (Photo 2).

5 Place a small section of brown tape on the stripes that are not being painted to help you remember which stripes to avoid.

6 If a painted stripe would butt up at the corner of the room with another painted stripe or if an unpainted stripe would butt up to another unpainted stripe, divide the last stripe in half, in effect creating two narrow stripes in its place. Otherwise, take a few inches (5 to 7 cm) off the last few stripes. You will never notice the difference in spacing, especially when the stripes meet in an inconspicuous corner.

Photo 1. Mark the location of the vertical lines with chalk.

Photo 2. Draw the vertical lines with chalk, using the level.

Photo 3. Tape the stripes, several at a time.

Photo 4. Glaze the stripes with a brush.

Photo 5. Pull off the brown tape around the vertical stripes.

Taping the Vertical Stripes

1 Tape off the trim surrounding the area to be painted, using blue tape, to protect it.

2 Define the sides of a few stripes at a time with tape, using brown paper tape (Photo 3).

3 Lay the drop cloth out under the first wall you plan on painting.

Painting the Vertical Stripes

1 Apply the Summer Sun glaze with a brush, using up-and-down or vertical strokes (Photo 4) as shown.

2 Pull off the brown tape after each stripe is painted, or after a few are painted (Photo 5).

3 Finish each wall in the same manner.

tip

Tape off 2 or 3 stripes at a time, and then paint them. If you tape off more than 2 or 3, the tape may begin to peel off, and you'll end up doing the taping twice.

INSTRUCTIONS FOR PLAID, DAY 2

Marking the Horizontal Stripes

1 Begin in a corner. Starting at the ceiling, measure down 8" (20 cm) or 12" (30.5 cm) if you are painting a larger wall, and mark with chalk (Photo 6).

2 Continue measuring and marking until you reach the bottom of the wall.

3 Using the level, draw the lines with chalk horizontally across the wall (Photo 7).

4 Place a small section of brown tape on the stripe that is not being painted to help you remember which areas to paint.

Photo 6. Measure down 8" (20 cm) from the ceiling.

Photo 7. Draw the horizontal lines with chalk, using the level.

Photo 8. Tape off the stripes.

Photo 9. Paint on the glaze using a brush.

Photo 10. Pull off the brown tape.

Taping Off and Glazing the Horizontal Stripes

1 Lay the drop cloth out under the first wall you plan to paint.

2 Using the brown paper tape, tape off the first few stripes at the top of the wall (Photo 8).

3 Apply the glaze with a brush to the first stripe down, painting in a horizontal direction between the tape edges (Photo 9).

4 Pull off the brown tape after a few stripes have been painted (Photo 10).

5 Continue taping off and painting the stripes, as you did with the vertical stripes.

6 Pull off the blue tape that is protecting the trim after one whole wall is complete. You can see the finished plaid on page 68.

tip

If you apply glaze with a brush, you will get a noticeable brushstroke in the plaid. This woven effect looks great in the areas on the wall where horizontal and vertical stripes overlap.

73

plaid

more plaids

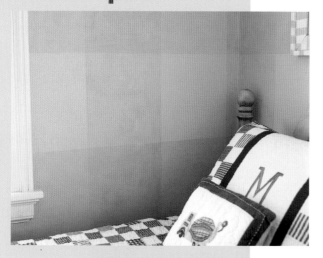

A light blue base color is glazed with a darker blue to create a simple check pattern from horizontal and vertical stripes. Where the glazes intersect, a darker square is formed, an effect that's easier to obtain with glaze than with flat paint since glaze is transparent. You can try this pattern with any tonal color scheme. The 12"-wide (30.5 cm) blue stripes were created by washing on Sunny's Goodtime Marine Glaze.

above left and right: A mix of colors on a small piece of furniture gives instant personality to any room. Plaids turn this run-of-the-mill dresser into a one-of-a-kind piece. The gold border and gold knobs add a distinctive finishing detail. The base color is latex flat white. The plaid was created in green, pink, blue, and tan acrylic artist's paints. Sunny's Goodtime Metallic Gold was used on the knobs and edges. The entire piece was glazed with Sunny's Goodtime Original Aging Glaze.

Mix and match plaid with other patterns in similar color schemes. The busyness of this dresser is all-of-a-piece, which is why it works. The basecoat is chartreuse green. The plaid was created in various oil flat colors: brown, blue, yellow, green, peach, and black. The entire piece was aged with raw umber artist's tube oil mixed with Old Masters Tinting Glaze, applied with a rag.

tip

Use a plaid pattern to create a focal-point wall, rather than painting an entire room.

Since this room has bold curtains, we used a narrow line of pink on the inside of the panel and a wider line of brown on the outside in order to balance the color. The inside of the panel is glazed a shade darker than the wall color to add depth and interest.

panels

what you need:

- ◆ **Baseboard: warm yellow paint (Benjamin Moore latex eggshell 2020-50 in model)**
- ◆ **Brown paint (Benjamin Moore latex flat HC-76 in model)**
- ◆ **Rose paint (Benjamin Moore latex flat 1360 in model)**
- ◆ **Warm glaze: Sunny's Goodtime Summer Sun Glaze combination color (20 oz. Sunshine Daydream Glaze + 4 oz. Original Aging Glaze) in model**
- ◆ **24" (61 cm) plastic level with ruler**
- ◆ **Tape measure and chalk**
- ◆ **2" (5 cm) brown paper tape**
- ◆ **1" (2.5 cm) blue painter's tape for trim**
- ◆ **Synthetic bristle artist's brush, size 10**
- ◆ **White cotton T-shirt or rag**
- ◆ **Drop cloth**
- ◆ **Ladder**

ADDING PANELS to a room creates art on your wall space. Panels can be as simple or intricate as you desire. Vertical panels turn a plain wall into a work of art itself, and change an otherwise empty wall into the perfect spot for paintings, mirrors, or other works of art.

Panels also draw the eye upward and make ceilings appear higher. They break up unusually large walls and give the effect of a formal ballroom or living room to spaces with little furnishing. Where previously there was empty space, a classically decorative hall appears.

To keep the room balanced in terms of height and width, place all the panels equidistant from the corners and doorways, as well as from the ceiling and chair rail or baseboard.

right and opposite: The base color is a light yellow-orange, Benjamin Moore latex eggshell 2020-50. The ¼" (6 mm) inner outline was done in rose, Benjamin Moore latex eggshell 1360, and the ½" (1.3 cm) outer outline was done in brown, Benjamin Moore latex eggshell HC-76.

Prior to starting the panels, basecoat the walls (in our model, warm yellow paint was used). Let dry for a week.

INSTRUCTIONS FOR PANELS

Measuring and Painting Panels

1 For each panel, measure down an equal distance (6" to 8" or 15 to 20 cm) from each corner of the ceiling and mark a horizontal line with chalk. Also measure in the same distance from both sides of the panel's wall, and draw a vertical chalk line to mark this distance (Photo 1).

2 Measure up the same distance from the baseboard and mark the line in chalk.

3 Start to tape off the panel, aligning the bottom of the tape on the chalk line (Photo 2).

4 Continue taping off in the same way to create vertical outlines for your panel (Photo 3).

5 Apply the glaze with a rag inside the taped area of the panel (Photo 4).

6 For this panel, we then taped off a ¼" (6 mm) border (Photo 5) by adding a second line of tape ¼" inside the first line, after the glaze was dry.

7 Paint the inner border lines pink with a small artist's brush (Photo 6). An outer brown ½" (1.3 cm) border was added later; you can see it in the finished panel over my left shoulder.

Photo 1. Measure 6" to 8" (15 to 20 cm) in from the edge of the panel and mark a vertical chalk line.

Photo 2. Tape along the horizontal chalk line with the bottom of the tape aligned on the chalk line.

Photo 3. Tape along the vertical chalk line with the inner edge of the tape aligned on the chalk line to define the side of the panel.

tip

Glaze the walls around painted
panels for a dramatic effect.

8 Once the inner border is dry, remove the inner round
of tape (Photo 7).

9 For the rest of the panels in your design, proceed as
for the panel described above.

10 For the outer, brown border, mark chalk lines a few
inches (5 to 7 cm) out from the first border, and put
tape lines on both sides of the border space as you did
for the inner border; however, leave a ½" (1.3 cm)
space between the tape lines instead of a ¼" (6 mm)
space for the paint. Use the small artist's brush to paint
the brown border. When everything is dry, remove
tape. The finished room can be seen on page 76.

Photo 4. Apply the glaze with a rag to the whole panel.

Photo 5. Place tape ¼" (6 mm) in to define the narrow pink outline.

Photo 6. Paint the pink border between the tapes.

Photo 7. Remove the inner round of tape once the pink border is dry.

more panels

Multiple thin lines define these panels. The green and red lines tie in to the other decorative elements in the room. The walls were first painted a light green, and then the panels were painted light cream. Once the main panels were in place, the colored lines were added for both color and dimension, yielding a trompe l'oeil result. The green lines add definition, and the ruby red lines add a dramatic accent. The panel outlining was done in Sunny's Goodtime Ruby Red Glaze and Gator Green Glaze.

The multistriped rug and painted furniture in this room cry out for something unconventional. I measured 6" (15 cm) down from the crown molding and 6" up from the baseboard to mark lines for the top and bottom of each panel. Then I measured 6" in from the perpendicular wall on each side to establish the panel size. The walls were painted green and then the panel was washed an aqua blue. To bring down the brightness, I washed another light blue on top of the aqua. For the panel borders, I originally painted a straight 1½" (4 cm) coral border, but it looked a little harsh, so I cut a small flower stencil and used the original green base paint to stencil over the coral line and break up the color. Stenciling with the green on top of the coral softens and customizes the look. The base color is a pale celadon green. The panels were washed with Sunny's Goodtime Bahama Blue Colour Wash. The second wash is Sunny's Goodtime Little Boy Blue Colour Wash.

Panels in this room break up the wall space and provide frames for the pair of demi-lune tables on either side of the fireplace. For panel outlines, I usually paint a very thin line of the darkest color, in this case brown, and a thicker line in a lighter shade, here pink. A thin line of gold just outside the pink gilds the panel frame. The base color is a medium yellow. The pink outline is 2" (5 cm) wide. The brown outline is ¼" (6 mm) wide.

The panels in this dining room are trimmed with multiple gold lines to echo the elegant furnishings and lighting. The flat white paint in the center of the panel evens out the other whites used in the room. The base color is a pale blue-gray. The panels were painted in white and outlined in a light gray. The gold lines are Sunny's Goodtime Metallic Gold Stencil Paint.

83

A stoneblock pattern assimilates easily in this elegant foyer and exudes a sense of history. The neutral earth tones work well with the décor in the adjoining rooms. The base color is Benjamin Moore latex eggshell Linen White. The stoneblocks were done in Sunny's Goodtime Original Aging Glaze, washed on with a rag.

stoneblock

what you need:

- Basecoat: White paint (Benjamin Moore latex eggshell White in model)
- Stoneblock: Warm tan glaze (Sunny's Goodtime Paint Original Aging Glaze in model)
- Measuring tape
- 24" (61 cm) plastic level with ruler
- ½" (1.3 cm) white artist's tape (thin tape available in art supply stores)
- 1" (2.5 cm) blue painter's tape for trim
- Chalk
- 2½" (6.5 cm) natural bristle brush
- White cotton T-shirt or rag
- Drop cloth
- Ladder

REAL STONE is expensive and perhaps too heavy for your home interior, but painted stone finish lets you capture the feel of natural materials, which you might not otherwise be able to have.

Less busy than a plaid and less ornate than a series of panels, stoneblock can be casual in a child's room or formal in an entry hall. A 24" by 12" (61 cm by 30.5 cm) block is classic.

The basic concept of stoneblock is simple. Walls are painted an off-white color. Rectangles imitating large stone blocks are marked on the walls you want to decorate, starting from the top down. Then the outlines of the rectangles are protected by thin tape while a stone-colored glaze is rubbed on. When the tape is removed, the unpainted areas simulate the mortar that holds real stone blocks together.

Warm stoneblock pattern on a test board. The base color is white. The stoneblocks were done in Sunny's Goodtime Palm Beach Pink Colour Wash.

Photo 1. At top, one round of stoneblocks is already marked and glazed. Draw a horizontal line around the room 12" (30.5 cm) down from the previous line, using the level.

Photo 2. Draw the vertical marks at 24" (61 cm) intervals to mark a row of blocks all around the room.

INSTRUCTIONS FOR STONEBLOCK

Marking the Horizontal Lines for Stoneblock

1 Choose an inconspicuous corner where the patterns will meet, in case blocks get cut off later on. This should be an area that you don't view immediately upon walking into the room.

2 Measure 12" (30.5 cm) down from the line where the ceiling meets a wall, and mark the 12" distance with a chalk dot.

3 Using the level, continue measuring and marking 12" (30.5 cm) down from the ceiling line around any walls you plan to do in stoneblock.

4 Using the level, draw a horizontal line to connect the row of chalk marks you just made 12" down, all around the room. The horizontal lines should align at each corner. In Photo 1 the top round of stoneblocks already has been marked, taped, and glazed, and the author is measuring the second round.

5 Continue measuring downward and marking 12" (30.5 cm) distances between horizontal lines. Then use the level to connect the chalk marks. Draw all the horizontal lines needed to fill your wall.

Marking the Vertical Lines for Stoneblock

1 After you have marked your horizontal lines, measure around the top horizontal line and mark chalk dots at 24" (61 cm) intervals.

2 Using the level, draw vertical lines from the chalk dots you just made down to the next horizontal chalk line

(Photo 2). This will demarcate the row of blocks on the wall, each of which will be 24" (61 cm) wide and 12" (30.5 cm) deep.

3 For the second row of blocks, start 12" (30.5 cm) in from the side edge of the block above it and mark a vertical line. Then measure horizontally 24" (61 cm) to mark the next vertical line. Skipping the first 12" on the horizontal line means that the blocks will align in a staggered pattern (see Photo 8 for example). Continue measuring horizontally and marking dots with chalk at 24" (61 cm) intervals around the room on the second row.

4 Using the level, draw vertical lines where the chalk dots are to make the second row.

5 For the remaining rows, use the level to mark lines as before, spacing each new vertical line 12" (30.5 cm) away from the previous vertical line above it. Use the vertical lines from the first row as reference in order to space the lines for the third row, and so on.

6 If the stoneblock at the end of the row is too big or too small, add the block's width and the width of the previous block and divide the result in two to make two narrower-than-usual or two wider-than-usual blocks of equal width.

Taping Off the Lines before Glazing for Stoneblock

1 First tape off all the horizontal lines with the white artist's tape (Photo 3), and then tape all the vertical lines (Photo 4).

2 Use 1" (2.5 cm) wide blue painter's tape on any moldings and baseboards to protect them.

Photo 3. Cover the horizontal chalk lines with thin white artist's tape.

Photo 4. Cover all the vertical lines with artist's tape too.

Photo 5. Apply the glaze with a brush and rub it in with a rag.

Photo 6. Continue to apply the glaze and rub it in.

Glazing the Stoneblock

1 Brush the glaze on and rub it with a rag as though you were cleaning the walls. Use a colorwash or an aging glaze tinted a neutral color like off-white or beige, depending on the room (Photos 5 and 6).

2 To keep paint from bleeding under the tape, glaze 3 or 4 blocks at a time and promptly remove the tape after painting (Photo 7).

Photo 7. Remove the tape promptly after glazing.

Photo 8. With a rag, carefully remove any excess paint that seeped under the tape.

3 Using a rag, carefully remove any paint that may have seeped under the tape (Photo 8).

4 The line that the artist's tape covered looks like the mortar between the blocks when the tape is removed. See page 84 for the completed stoneblock.

tip

Apply glaze in the center of the stoneblock and rub outward to avoid having glaze bleed under the tape.

more stoneblock

above and opposite: Stoneblocks in this charming child's room bring to mind a medieval castle. The base color is white. The stoneblocks were done in Sunny's Goodtime Original Aging Glaze, washed on with a cheesecloth.

Diamonds enliven a wall in my mud room. The base color is a light gray, Benjamin Moore latex eggshell 975. The diamonds were painted in yellow-green and light green, Benjamin Moore latex eggshell 391 and 536.

diamond walls

what you need:

HAND-PAINTED DIAMONDS on the walls create lively and distinctive rooms. The pattern requires measuring and drawing, but the result is impressive. The bigger the diamond, the more it opens the room and the more forgiving it is to mark out. Use brights for cheerful results and tonal colors if you want a more sophisticated look.

Paint each diamond a different color for fun in a child's room or kitchen. Use a tonal set of colors for a more sophisticated look in an entrance hall or bath. Get creative and outline diamonds with a third color, or add stencils at the intersections of diamonds.

Colorful diamonds have stenciled dots accentuating their corners.

Photo 1. Measure down 16" (or whatever your diagonal is) and make a second A mark below the first one for the lowest point of the first diamond.

Photo 2. Mark the center of the diamond.

Before starting the diamonds, basecoat the walls (in our model, light gray paint was used). Let dry for a week.

INSTRUCTIONS FOR DIAMOND WALLS
Marking the Diamond Points

1 Decide on the number of diamonds you want to put vertically on your wall, generally 3 to 6 depending on ceiling height. Here we are making 4 diamonds in a vertical column, and our diamonds started up at the top of the wall.

2 Measure the height of the wall and divide by the desired number of diamonds. That number, X, will be the height of the diagonal of the diamond (from point to opposite point, as our diamonds are squares set on the diagonal). Our diamonds had a diagonal of 16" (40.5 cm).

3 Beginning in an inconspicuous corner at the top left of the wall, measure across half the length of the diagonal (in this case 8") and make a small A with chalk for the top of the diamond. If you want there to be a space at the left of your diamonds, start to measure half the length of the diagonal a few inches to the right of the perpendicular wall.

4 With the level, measure 16" (40.5 cm) down the wall and make another A (Photo 1). This will mark the bottom point of the first diamond on the upper left. Continue making diamonds down the entire wall. If the measurements do not work out evenly at the bottom, add or subtract a bit on each side, or make part of a diamond.

5 Go back to the place where you marked the first A, measure down 8" (half of the diagonal's length), and mark that location. It will be the middle of the diamond (Photo 2). With your level, mark a point 8" (20 cm, or half the diagonal's length) to the left of the middle with a B and also mark a B 8" to the right of the diamond's middle. These will be the left and right points of the first diamond on the upper left. Finish the rest of the diamonds in that left column the same way.

Photo 3. Continue measuring and marking across to situate diamonds.

6 Next, measure 16" (40.5 cm) across the wall, starting from the first A you marked, and mark the new place with another A. Each A will be a top point of a new diamond. Continue marking across the entire wall the same way, or as far as you want.

7 Go back to the position where you marked the first B (the left point of the first diamond), measure down 16" (40.6 cm), and mark this position with a B. This will be the leftmost point of the second diamond under the first one you drew. Measure 16" across the wall and mark with another B. This will be the rightmost point of the second diamond down.

8 Continue measuring and marking down and across the wall with A and B marks to make as many diamonds as you need (Photo 3).

9 Use this measurement method for the rest of the walls of the room.

tips

* Another way to mark diamonds on a wall is to cut a cardboard square to the size you need for the diamond and trace around it as is done for the diamond floor (see page 102) using a pencil that matches your paint color.

* You can also draw and paint diamonds that are longer from the top to the bottom point than they are across.

Photo 4. Tape the edges of the diamond from A to B, with the inner edge of the tape defining the limits of the diamond.

Photo 5. Paint from the center of each diamond out to the edge of the tape.

Taping Off the Diamonds

1 Tape off the trim and ceiling using the blue painter's tape to protect them from paint.

2 Lay the drop cloth out under the wall you plan to paint.

3 Now it's a matter of connecting the A points and B points. Using the brown tape, tape from the first A down to the first B on its left. The inner side of the tape should fall on the diagonal line between them. In a similar manner, tape from that B diagonally down to the next A. Then tape the right side of the diamond in the same way (Photo 4).

4 Start at the top of the wall and work your way down. In Photo 4 we see me taping from the A at the top of a diamond down to the B on the right of the diamond.

5 Tape off every other column of diamonds in the same way, using the A points for the tops and bottoms of the diamonds and the B points for the side points of the diamonds.

Painting the Diamonds on the Wall

1 Using a brush, put paint in the center of the taped-off diamond and paint out to the tape edges to prevent paint from bleeding under the tape (Photo 5).

2 Remove the tape promptly after applying the paint (Photo 6).

3 Plan your color scheme so you know which colors go where. In chalk, tag the diamonds you need to paint with

Photo 6. Remove the tape.

the color they will be to avoid confusion. Begin painting the second column of taped-off diamonds. If you have a large wall to paint, it is helpful to skip a diamond between the one you just painted and the next one you need to paint, so the nearby wet paint doesn't get smudged.

4 After going around the room in this manner, you will have painted half the diamonds that are supposed to be painted.

5 After the first set of diamond columns dries, start the second round of taping and painting in the remaining columns of diamonds you wish to paint.

6 The chalk marks can be cleaned with a damp rag after all the painting is done and it has dried for 24 hours. The finished diamonds can be seen on page 92.

tips

* Use tonal colors and add a small design at the intersections.

* If your time is limited, do one wall every few days or so.

* Glaze or colorwash diamonds using two shades: one light and one darker shade of the same color.

more diamond walls

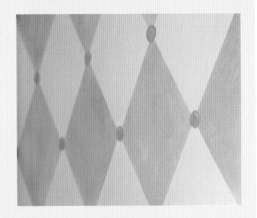

To update an older bathroom, we chose a diamond pattern in the same color as the tiles and accented the diamonds with dots in the intersections. The three-color rule is at work again. The base color is white. The diamonds were done in Sunny's Goodtime combination color (6 oz. Black Leather Glaze + 18 oz. French Gray Colour Wash), washed on with a cheesecloth. Sunny's Goodtime Metallic Gold Stencil Paint was sponged onto Sunny's Goodtime Dot Stencil.

The large floor-to-ceiling diamonds in a neutral color add some fun, yet keep things simple. This is a nice idea for a child's room, a long hallway, or an office area. The subtle color difference is achieved by applying glaze with cheesecloth. The base color is pale beige. Sunny's Goodtime Original Aging Glaze was applied with a rag to create the diamonds.

above and opposite: This floor was inspired by a magazine clipping. To achieve the same light, airy feeling, we first painted on the diamonds and then glazed the floor, which also helps keep every speck of dirt from showing up. This floor works in the entry hall and extends beautifully to the living and dining rooms and den. The diamonds were painted in Benjamin Moore Floor & Patio satin latex enamel Cliffside Gray and White (thinned down). The diamonds were outlined using the same paint in Platinum Gray.

diamond floor

what you need:

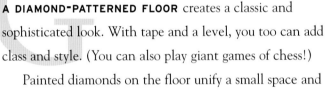

A **DIAMOND-PATTERNED FLOOR** creates a classic and sophisticated look. With tape and a level, you too can add class and style. (You can also play giant games of chess!)

Painted diamonds on the floor unify a small space and lighten and brighten a large space. Diamonds can make floors in a newer home look established, and they can refresh older floors as well. They can be kept simple, or they can be outlined, aged, and embellished. Basic or ornate, they're a fun and stylish alternative to carpets and linoleum. Large diamonds look even better in small spaces. Not only do they open up the room, but they're less busy and much easier to mark out in your preparation stages.

- ◆ White enamel paint (Benjamin Moore's Floor & Patio satin latex enamel in model) for basecoat
- ◆ Gray enamel paint (Benjamin Moore's Floor & Patio Cliffside Gray satin latex enamel in model) for diamonds
- ◆ Platinum gray paint (Benjamin Moore's Floor & Patio satin latex in model) for outlines
- ◆ Sunny's Goodtime Aging Glaze
- ◆ 2 1/2" (6.5 cm) natural bristle brush
- ◆ Flat artist's paintbrush, about 1/2" (1 cm) wide
- ◆ Cotton T-shirt or rag
- ◆ Blue painter's tape
- ◆ Artist's canvas stretched and mounted on a frame cut to the size of your diamonds. The frame shown here is 30" by 30" (76 by 76 cm).
- ◆ Colored pencil that matches paint color
- ◆ Extendable metal measuring tape
- ◆ Plastic level with ruler
- ◆ Chalk

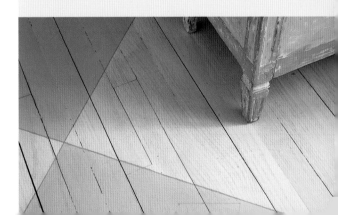

1

2

INSTRUCTIONS FOR DIAMOND FLOOR

Preparing the Diamond Floor

1 Preparation is key for wood floors. Before you spend precious time painting your design, hire a professional to have the floors sanded and sealed with one coat of poly-acrylic. The polyacrylic coat ensures that the paint will not seep into the wood floor, so that if you ever want to have them sanded back to wood you may do so.

2 Once the floor has been properly prepared, paint it with a latex floor paint (white in the model). Benjamin Moore Floor & Patio paint works well. It is possible to get this custom-made in latex satin enamel.

Note: Our demonstration was done on a plywood floor. For concrete, vinyl, or other types of floor, consult with a paint store for recommendations on the proper base primer for your surface.

Marking the Diamonds

1 First, measure to find the center of the floor in the room that you are painting. Draw chalk lines from the middle of each wall across the room; they will cross in the center. Mark the center spot with a colored pencil. This is where you will begin tracing a diamond, which will be centered over this spot.

2 The square of canvas was our template for tracing these diamonds. Place the center of the canvas square on the

Photo 1. For accuracy, measure out from the wall to the side point of the diamond in hard-to-reach places.

Photo 2. Measure and mark the other side point in the same way.

Place a stencil at each diamond intersection to create another floor pattern.

center dot you drew earlier, with the points aligned on the chalk lines to make sure it is centered. Centering your first diamond in the middle of the floor will ensure that all the rest of the diamonds are positioned well throughout the room.

3 Line up each new diamond by placing the canvas frame next to the previously drawn diamond, aligning the diamonds point to point at the side. Check with the level or tape measure that the top and bottom points of the canvas diamond are aligned horizontally with the previously drawn diamond. Continue adding diamonds up and down the room and then across.

4 Use a plastic level or tape measure to extend a straight line into hard-to-reach places where the canvas frame does not fit. Essentially, you are approximating with the tape measure what you'd draw if you were able to trace the frame.

5 Photos 1 and 2 show a diamond being drawn in a corner. Measure out from the wall with the tape measure to make sure that the two side points of the diamond frame are an equal distance from the wall. To do this, hold the canvas down firmly, by sitting on it if necessary, and mark the points (Photo 2).

6 Mark the diamond by tracing around the whole canvas frame with your pencil (Photos 3, 4 and 5).

Photos 3 through 5. Trace around the frame in pencil.

3

4

5

103

6

7

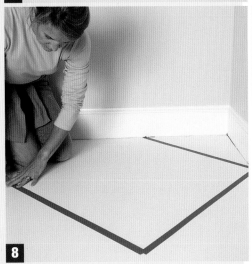

8

9

7 After tracing, tape around all the diamonds to be painted with blue painter's tape (Photos 6 to 9). The inner edge of the tape should align with the pencil lines you drew; the pencil line should be visible just inside the tape.

Painting the Diamonds

1 Apply the gray paint near the center of the diamond with the wide brush, and work outward to the edges of the tape. I used an acrylic floor paint for our model.

2 Once the diamond is dry, remove the tape. Add a new line of blue painter's tape just inside the edge of the gray diamond, with the tape's outer edge aligned with the edge of the gray diamond.

3 Add another line of tape a small distance out from the first line (Photo 10), for example, ¼" (6 mm).

4 With an artist's paintbrush, paint between the lines of tape you put down (Photo 11). I used dark platinum gray.

5 When the paint is dry, remove the tape (Photo 12).

Photos 6 through 9. Apply blue painter's tape to the diamond, aligning the inside of the tape with your pencil lines.

6 After all the diamonds and outlines have dried for a week, apply an aging glaze to the entire floor. The way to do this is to put down some glaze with a paintbrush and then spread it with a cotton rag, working a small area at a time (Photo 13).

7 Hire a professional to apply an acrylic or oil top coat, at least two coats. Consult with your floor sander when the floors are being prepared as to whether you want to use a water-based or polyurethane top coat, keeping in mind that polyurethane will yellow over time. The finished floor can be seen on page 100.

Photo 10. Preparing to paint a thin border by putting 2 lines of tape around the gray diamond: one with its outer edge flush with the edge of the gray diamond and the second a small distance out from the first line of tape.

Photo 11. Starting to paint the thin border.

Photo 12. Removing the tape once the thin border has been painted.

Photo 13. Spreading an aging glaze all over the floor with a rag, after it has been applied with a paintbrush.

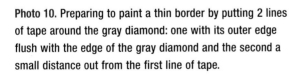

more diamond floors

This oak floor entry hall was sanded and sealed with one coat of polyacrylic before we started to paint. The diamonds were washed on first with thinned white paint to create the pattern. Then the entire floor was washed again with the same thinned white paint. When that dried, a brown outline was painted around the diamonds, and small circles added at the intersections in tan. When the outlines and circles were dry, the entire floor was glazed with Sunny's Goodtime Original Aging Glaze.

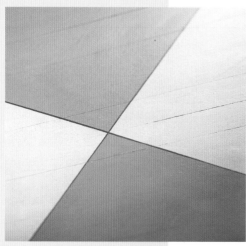

The defining feature of this dining room is the large-scale diamond pattern. The diamonds were outlined with a thin line of dark gray. The basecoat is a white latex satin enamel designed for floors. The diamonds were painted with latex satin enamel in gray. The diamond outlines were done with 50% gray and 50% black.

A painted floor that preserves the wood grain! The alternating diamonds were painted in white and outlined in brown latex satin enamel. The floor was then glazed for depth. Painted furniture and stained antiques are equally at home in this room.

Diamonds on Furniture

Mix and match diamonds with other patterns. The diamonds and hand-painted rooster complement the aged look of this country dresser and the wide green stripes of the walls.

This long, narrow bathroom is situated between two girls' rooms. The bedrooms are brightly colored, so black and white is a nice connecting thread. The freehand flower pattern is fun and sophisticated at the same time.

freehand

what you need:

- ◆ **Palette paper or wax paper**
- ◆ **#10 synthetic artist's brush**
- ◆ **Black acrylic artist's tube paint (or color of your choice)**
- ◆ **Chalk**
- ◆ **Ladder**
- ◆ **Cotton T-shirt or rag**
- ◆ **Drop cloth**
- ◆ **Cardboards for testing designs**

FREEHAND IS THE ULTIMATE in decorative self-expression. Even if you haven't drawn anything since grade school, give it a try. You may choose flowers, abstract patterns, squiggles, or curlicues to liven up your space. Freehand is easier if you trace the pattern out beforehand with chalk.

You can freehand on walls, borders, panels, or furniture. I use a round #10 synthetic brush, because it allows me to control how wide or thin I want a line to be.

Practice making freehand designs with your brush and some water on a piece of cardboard first, before you use paint on a wall.

Unusual color combinations give any design or pattern a totally new look. Try robin's egg blue with red, or magenta with gray.

Freehand vine pattern. The base color is a pale blue. The freehand design was done in a light brown. The entire piece was aged with Sunny's Goodtime Ocean Age Aging Glaze.

MARKING OUT THE DESIGN
AND PAINTING FOR FREEHAND

1 Draw your desired design with the chalk (Photo 1).

2 Use a paper palette to load your brush with black paint
(Photo 2); then paint the design on top of the chalk lines.
You can see the hand position in Photos 3 and 4.

3 Chalk marks can be cleaned with a damp rag after the room is
completed and the paint has had 24 hours to dry (Photo 5).

Photo 1. Drawing the design with chalk.

Photo 2. Loading the brush.

Photo 3 and 4. Starting to paint; notice the hand position.

Photo 5. Cleaning up chalk marks.

more freehand

I drew the rope border freehand with chalk in this little boy's room and then glazed the bottom two-thirds of the wall. I painted the rope white first and then added the blue. The circles on top of each point ground the design, and the white highlight gives it dimension. The base color of the wall is green. Sunny's Goodtime Fern combination color (4 oz. Original Aging Glaze + 20 oz. Gator Green Glaze) was washed on with a rag below the freehand border.

This freehand flower-and-vine border is lower than standard borders, about 14" (35 cm) from the ceiling. The base color of the walls is a pale yellow. Sunny's Goodtime Cantaloupe combination color (12 oz. Pumpkin Glaze + 12 oz. Sunshine Daydream Glaze) was washed on with a rag below the freehand border. The border was done in Sunny's Goodtime Fern Glaze, Ruby Red Glaze, and Pumpkin Glaze.

left: A wavy stripe on plain white walls is cheerful and easy as pie. The lines are spaced 17" (43 cm) apart. The base color of the walls is white. The stripes were done in a lime green. The dots were done in Sunny's Goodtime Cantaloupe combination color (12 oz. Pumpkin Glaze + 12 oz. Sunshine Daydream Glaze) and Sunny's Goodtime Bubblegum combination color (16 oz. Palm Beach Pink Colour Wash + 8 oz. Ruby Red Glaze).

below: Doorknobs are a great center for a freehand flower of any sort. The vine was painted in a light green, and the flower was painted in a medium rose. The doorknob was done in a light orange.

left: Freehand colored circles on a neutral background tie in with the green tile in this bathroom. The trim is painted the same color as the edging tile. The base color of the walls is white. Sunny's Goodtime Cappuccino Glaze, a light gray glaze, was washed on with a rag. The circles were painted in a medley of colors: yellow, purple, orange, green, and a reddish pink.

freehand canopy

A canopy adds style to a room that doesn't have crown moldings or other architectural elements to distinguish the walls from the ceiling. The idea is to create a visual covering for the room by painting a freehand border that connects the top wall portion with the ceiling. The ceiling is painted the same color as the uppermost portion of the wall; colorwashing the walls below the border also contributes to the canopy effect. Here are some tips for making canopies:

• Chalk the border approximately 14" to 16" (35 to 40.5 cm) below the ceiling.

• Colorwash the lower walls before painting the border.

• Plain dots are easy to draw freehand.

• Stencils also work in a canopy design, but keep them simple.

Everything in this room was painted taupe first, including the ceiling. I drew the border with chalk. Then I washed the walls up to the chalk border with Sunny's Goodtime French Gray Colour Wash and used a warm terra-cotta glaze on top of that (Sunny's Goodtime Take Me to Tuscany Glaze); both were washed on with rags. The freehand scroll border and the stenciled dots were done on the canopy and ceiling in the same French gray.

This whimsical canopy pulls in the colors of the existing fabrics. The green dots from the curtains and bed linens find their way to the ceiling and border. The walls are washed a darker color than the ceiling to weight the room. The base color is white. Sunny's Goodtime Bubblegum Pink Glaze combination color (16 oz. Palm Beach Pink Colour Wash + 8 oz. Ruby Red Glaze) was washed on the walls with a rag. Sunny's Goodtime Dot Stencil was done in light lime green. The freehand border was painted in a bright pink.

glossary of paint terms

aging glaze: a glaze applied to walls, furniture, or floors to give the appearance of age.

bristles: the working part of a brush, which may be natural (usually hog hair) or artificial (nylon or polyester).

clearcoat: a transparent protective and/or decorative film.

colorwash: a thin, high-pigment water-based paint that is made to be applied by literally washing your walls; it gives a watery fresco effect.

durability: the ability of paint to last or hold up well upon exposure to destructive agents such as weather, sunlight, detergents, abrasion, and marring.

eggshell: the degree of gloss between flat and semi-gloss finish.

enamel: a broad classification of paints that dry to a hard finish; they may be flat, semi-gloss, or high-gloss and can be water- or oil-based.

exterior: the outside surfaces of a structure.

fading: the loss of color caused by exposure to light, heat, and weathering.

flat: a paint surface that scatters or absorbs the light falling on it so as to be substantially free from gloss or sheen.

glaze: transparent, often tinted finish, applied over a painted surface to add the illusion of texture, create interest, or soften the original color.

gloss: the luster or shininess of paints and coatings.

interior: the inside surfaces of a structure.

latex-based paint: a general term for water-based emulsion paint, such as polyvinyl acetate, styrene butadiene, and acrylic.

metallics: a class of paints that include metal flakes in their composition.

oil-based paints: those made with drying oil and mineral spirits or paint thinner; they generally dry very hard but take longer to dry than latex paints and require more time to recoat.

pigments: paint ingredients mainly used to impart color and hiding power.

polyacrylic: a water-based protective top coat, usually non-yellowing. Can only be used with water-based paints.

polyurethane: a kind of paint with an oil base; it comes in a wide range of coatings, ranging from hard gloss enamels to soft, flexible ones. Polyurethane takes longer to dry than polyacrylic and yellows with age. It can be used on top of either oil- or water-based paints.

primer: the first coat or undercoat that helps to bind the top coat to the substrate; such paints are designed to provide adequate adhesion to new surfaces or are formulated to meet the special requirements of the surfaces.

ragging: a technique for applying glaze to create texture.

semi-gloss: a finish with a low-luster sheen between flat and full gloss.

shellac: derived from a resinous substance called lac that is formed on certain Asian trees; it is alcohol-based and is used as a sealer and finish for floors, for sealing knots, and for other purposes.

sheen: the degree of luster of a dried paint film, generally classified as flat, matte, eggshell, semi-gloss, or high-gloss.

stippling: tapping a paintbrush lightly and vertically to gain coverage into crevices.

tack: sticky condition of coating during drying, between the wet and dry-to-touch stages.

texture: the roughness or irregularity of a surface.

undercoat: a primer or intermediate coating before the finish coating.

varnish: transparent liquid that dries on exposure to air to give a decorative or protective coating when applied as a thin film.

water-based coatings: those in which most of the liquid content is water.

paint information for photos

Basics section:

page 2: The base color is a green, Benjamin Moore latex eggshell 2028-60. The inside panels were washed with Sunny's Goodtime Bahama Blue Colour Wash and then with Sunny's Goodtime Little Boy Blue Colour Wash. The 1½" (4 cm) outline of the panels was done in coral, Benjamin Moore latex eggshell 2009-30, and a small flower stencil in the original green was stenciled over it.

page 4, top: The base color is a medium yellow (Farrow & Ball latex eggshell 218). The 2" (5 cm) panel outline was done in pink, Benjamin Moore latex eggshell 1360. The ¼" (6 mm) panel outline was done in brown, Benjamin Moore latex eggshell HC-76.

page 4, bottom: The urn was painted in Benjamin Moore oil high-gloss 399.

page 5, top and bottom: The cabinet was painted in a light blue-gray, Farrow & Ball oil flat 82. The entire piece was aged with Old Masters Tinting Glaze mixed with Winsor & Newton's artist's tube oil in raw umber.

page 6, top and bottom: The base color is Benjamin Moore latex eggshell Linen White. The 12"-wide (30.5 cm) stripes were done in gray-blue, Benjamin Moore 1632, mixed with Sunny's Goodtime Clear Glaze. The ¼"-wide (6 mm) stripes were done in a medium brown, Benjamin Moore HC-69. The whole wall was washed with Sunny's Goodtime Cappuccino Glaze.

page 7, top and bottom: The base color is a taupe, Benjamin Moore latex eggshell HC-91. Sunny's Goodtime French Gray Colour Wash and Sunny's Goodtime Take Me to Tuscany Glaze (terra-cotta color) were washed on with rags below the scroll. The freehand scroll and Sunny's Goodtime Dot Stencil were both applied in Sunny's Goodtime French Gray Colour Wash.

page 8, top: The base color is a yellow, Benjamin Moore latex eggshell 2020-50. The ¼" (6 mm) panel outline is a light rose, Benjamin Moore latex eggshell 1360, and the ½" (1.3 cm) panel outline is a dark tan, Benjamin Moore latex eggshell HC-76.

page 8, bottom: The base color is a yellow-orange, Benjamin Moore latex eggshell 310. Stripes of several widths were painted in brown, pink, green, and a very light tan (Benjamin Moore HC-69, 1326, 405, and 944).

page 9, top: The base color is a light green, Benjamin Moore latex eggshell 542. Sunny's Goodtime Gator Green Glaze was washed on with a rag.

page 9, bottom: Stripes of varying widths were painted in three shades of orange: Benjamin Moore latex flat 083, 089, and 007.

page 10, top: The base color is a medium yellow (Farrow & Ball latex eggshell 218). The 2" (5 cm) panel outline was done in pink, Benjamin Moore latex eggshell 1360. The ¼" (6 mm) panel outline was done in brown, Benjamin Moore latex eggshell HC-76.

page 10, bottom: The base color is Benjamin Moore latex eggshell White. The stoneblocks were done in Sunny's Goodtime Original Aging Glaze, washed on with a cheesecloth.

page 11, top: The base color is a pale celadon green, Benjamin Moore latex eggshell 2028-60. The panels were washed with Sunny's Goodtime Bahama Blue Colour Wash. The second wash is Sunny's Goodtime Little Boy Blue Colour Wash. The narrow panel border was done in coral, Benjamin Moore latex eggshell 2009-30.

page 11, bottom: The base color is a pale beige, Benjamin Moore latex eggshell 1066. Sunny's Goodtime Original Aging Glaze was applied with a rag to create the diamonds.

page 12: The message-board wall was done with Benjamin Moore Chalkboard paint.

page 13: The walls were first painted a light green, Benjamin Moore latex eggshell 491, and then the panels were painted light cream, Benjamin Moore latex eggshell Linen White. The panel outlining was done in Sunny's Goodtime Ruby Red Glaze and Gator Green Glaze.

page 14, top: The base color is a pale green, Benjamin Moore latex eggshell 478. Sunny's Goodtime Fern Glaze combination color (4 oz. Original Aging Glaze + 20 oz. Gator Green Glaze) was washed on with a rag. Then Sunny's Goodtime Original Aging Glaze was sponged onto a custom-made stencil.

page 14, bottom: The base color is a medium ivory, Benjamin Moore latex eggshell 192. Sunny's Goodtime Apricot Colour Wash was washed on with a rag.

page 15, top: The base color of the walls is a pale yellow, Benjamin Moore latex eggshell HC-5. Sunny's Goodtime Cantaloupe combination color (12 oz. Pumpkin Glaze + 12 oz. Sunshine Daydream Glaze) was washed on with a rag below the free-hand border. The border was done in Sunny's Goodtime Fern Glaze, Ruby Red Glaze, and Pumpkin Glaze.

page 15, bottom: The base color is a light brown, Benjamin Moore latex eggshell HC-69. Sunny's Goodtime Black Leather Glaze was applied with a rag.

page 20, top: The diamonds were painted in Benjamin Moore Floor & Patio satin latex enamel Cliffside Gray and White (thinned down). The diamonds were outlined using the same paint in Platinum Gray.

page 20, bottom: The base color is a light gray, Benjamin Moore latex eggshell HC-173. The custom-made stencil was done in Sunny's Goodtime Bubblegum Pink Glaze combination color (16 oz. Palm Beach Pink + 8 oz. Ruby Red). The entire wall was aged in Sunny's Goodtime Original Aging Glaze, a brownish glaze, washed on with a rag.

page 21, top: The base color is a light blue-gray, Benjamin Moore latex eggshell 715. Sunny's Goodtime French Blue/Gray Glaze combination color (10 oz. Marine + 14 oz. Ocean Age Aging Glaze) was washed on the wall with a rag. Sunny's Goodtime Palm Stencil was sponged with white latex paint (Benjamin Moore Atrium White). Sunny's Goodtime Irregular Dot Stencil was sponged with Sunny's Goodtime Metallic Gold Stencil Paint.

page 21, bottom: The basecoat is Benjamin Moore latex eggshell Linen White. The wash is Sunny's Goodtime French Gray Colour Wash, and the glaze is Sunny's Goodtime Take Me to Tuscany, a warm, reddish brown.

page 22: The base color is Benjamin Moore latex eggshell White. Old Masters Tinting Glaze was tinted with

Winsor & Newton artist's tube oil paint in alizarin crimson. The oil glaze was rolled on and tapped with a cheesecloth.

page 24: The base color is a medium green, Benjamin Moore latex eggshell 391. Sunny's Goodtime Avocado Colour Wash (12 oz. Gator Green Glaze and 12 oz. Lizard Lime Colour Wash) was washed on with a rag.

Colorwash section:

page 25: The base color is a medium ivory, Benjamin Moore latex eggshell 192. Sunny's Goodtime Apricot Colour Wash was washed on with a rag.

page 27, top and bottom: The base color is a pale yellow, Benjamin Moore latex eggshell 289. 12 oz. of Sunny's Goodtime Buttercup Baby Colour Wash was mixed with 8 oz. of Sunny's Goodtime Apricot Colour Wash and washed on top.

page 28, top: The base color is a light green, Benjamin Moore latex eggshell 542. Sunny's Goodtime Gator Green Glaze was washed on with a rag.

page 28, bottom: The basecoat is Benjamin Moore latex eggshell Linen White. The wash is Sunny's Goodtime French Gray Colour Wash, and the glaze is Sunny's Goodtime Take Me to Tuscany, a warm, reddish brown.

page 29, top and bottom: Sunny's Goodtime Palm Beach Pink Colour Wash was colorwashed over a light taupe base (Benjamin Moore latex eggshell 944). The trim is Benjamin Moore oil semi-gloss Linen White, and the ceiling is pale pink (Benjamin Moore latex flat #884).

Stencil section:

page 30 and page 33: The base color is a taupe, Benjamin Moore latex eggshell 976. Sunny's Goodtime

Cantaloupe Glaze combination color (12 oz. Pumpkin Glaze + 12 oz. Sunshine Daydream Glaze) was washed on with a rag. The custom stencil was done in Sunny's Goodtime Bubblegum Pink Colour Wash (16 oz. Palm Beach Pink Colour Wash + 8 oz. Ruby Red Glaze).

page 31: The base color is a light blue-gray, Benjamin Moore latex eggshell 715. Sunny's Goodtime French Blue/Gray Glaze combination color (10 oz. Marine + 14 oz. Ocean Age Aging Glaze) was washed on the wall with a rag. Sunny's Goodtime Palm Stencil was sponged with white latex paint (Benjamin Moore Atrium White). Sunny's Goodtime Irregular Dot Stencil was sponged with Sunny's Goodtime Metallic Gold Stencil Paint.

page 34, left and right: The base color is a light pink, Benjamin Moore latex eggshell 1352. Sunny's Goodtime Rosey Rosey Glaze was washed on with a rag. The custom-made stencil was also done in Rosey Rosey Glaze. Sunny's Goodtime Original Aging Glaze was washed on top.

page 35, top: The base color is a pale green, Benjamin Moore latex eggshell 478. Sunny's Goodtime Fern Glaze combination color (4 oz. Original Aging Glaze + 20 oz. Gator Green Glaze) was washed on with a rag. Then Sunny's Goodtime Original Aging Glaze was sponged onto a custom-made stencil.

page 35, bottom: The base color is a light gray, Benjamin Moore latex eggshell HC-173. The custom-made stencil was done in Sunny's Goodtime Bubblegum Pink Glaze combination color (16 oz. Palm Beach Pink + 8 oz. Ruby Red). The entire wall was aged in Sunny's Goodtime Original Aging Glaze, a brownish glaze, washed on with a rag.

Glaze section:

page 36: The basecoat is a medium yellow (Farrow & Ball latex eggshell 218), and Sunny's Goodtime Summer Sun Glaze was painted on top.

page 37: The base color is a light brown, Benjamin Moore latex eggshell HC-69. Sunny's Goodtime Black Leather Glaze was applied with a rag.

page 40, top and bottom: The base color is Benjamin Moore latex eggshell White. Old Masters Tinting Glaze, tinted with Winsor & Newton artist's tube oil in alizarin crimson, was rolled on and then tapped with a cheesecloth.

page 41: The base color is a light tan, Benjamin Moore latex eggshell 1046. Sunny's Goodtime Original Aging Glaze was applied with a rag.

page 42, top and bottom: The base color is Benjamin Moore latex eggshell Linen White. Sunny's Goodtime Fern Glaze combination color (4 oz. Original Aging Glaze + 20 oz. Gator Green Glaze) was ragged on with a cheesecloth.

page 43, top and bottom: The wall base color is Benjamin Moore latex eggshell Muslin 1037. Sunny's Goodtime Original Aging Glaze was washed on top.

page 44, top and bottom: The base color is a beige, Benjamin Moore latex eggshell 1037. Sunny's Goodtime Original Aging Glaze was ragged on top.

page 45, top and bottom: The Venetian plaster is a Behr product, custom-mixed. It was tinted with hot pink.

Aging glaze section:

pages 46 and 47: The base color is a taupe, Benjamin Moore latex eggshell 976. Sunny's Goodtime Cantaloupe Glaze combination color (12 oz. Pumpkin + 12 oz. Sunshine

Daydream) was washed on with a rag. The custom-made stencil was done in Sunny's Goodtime Bubblegum Pink Glaze.

page 50, top left, and right: The base color is a warm light gray, Benjamin Moore oil Satin Impervo HC-173, and the highlights are a slightly darker warm gray, Benjamin Moore oil Satin Impervo HC-172. The entire chair was aged with Old Masters Tinting Glaze mixed with Winsor & Newton artist's tube oil in raw umber.

page 50, bottom left: The chair was first painted in a light tan, Benjamin Moore oil 1037, and then aged with Old Masters Tinting Glaze mixed with artist's tube oil in raw umber.

page 51, top and bottom: The cabinet was painted in a light blue-gray, Farrow & Ball oil flat 82. The entire piece was aged with Old Masters Tinting Glaze mixed with Winsor & Newton's artist's tube oil in raw umber.

page 52, top: The base color of the walls is a light blue-gray, Benjamin Moore latex eggshell HC-147. The ceiling color is one-half the wall formula. The furniture was painted in light blue-gray (Farrow & Ball latex flat 72) and aged with Sunny's Goodtime Original Aging Glaze.

page 52, bottom: The poles and finials were painted in a reddish brown, Benjamin Moore latex flat 1190, and then gilded with Mona Lisa Products Gold Leaf.

page 53, top: The cabinet was painted in a light gray, Benjamin Moore latex flat HC-172. The highlights were done in Sunny's Goodtime Metallic Gold Stencil Paint. The entire piece was aged with Sunny's Goodtime Original Aging Glaze.

page 53, bottom: The tables were painted in a chocolate brown, Benjamin Moore latex flat 1036. Sunny's Goodtime Black Leather Glaze was rubbed on top, and the

tables were gilded with Mona Lisa Products Gold Leaf.

Vertical stripes section:

pages 54 and 55: The base color is Benjamin Moore latex eggshell Decorators White. The 14"-wide (35 cm) green stripes were washed on in Sunny's Goodtime Avocado Colour Wash combination color (12 oz. Lizard Lime Colour Wash + 12 oz. Gator Green Glaze).

page 58, top: The basecoat is a light green, Benjamin Moore latex eggshell 2028-50, and the stripes are Sunny's Goodtime Gator Green Glaze.

page 58, bottom left and right: The base color is a pale yellow, Benjamin Moore latex eggshell 211. The 12"-wide (30.5 cm) stripes were washed on in Sunny's Goodtime Summer Sun Glaze combination color (4 oz. Original Aging Glaze + 20 oz. Sunshine Daydream Glaze). The stencil and darker stripe were done in Sunny's Summer Sun Glaze. Sunny's Goodtime Dot Stencil was done in Sunny's Metallic Gold Stencil Paint.

page 59, top and middle: The base color is Benjamin Moore latex eggshell Linen White. The 12"-wide (30.5 cm) stripes were done in gray-blue, Benjamin Moore 1632, mixed with Sunny's Goodtime Clear Glaze. The ¼"-wide (6 mm) stripes were done in a medium brown, Benjamin Moore HC-69. The whole wall was washed with Sunny's Goodtime Original Cappuccino Glaze.

page 59, bottom: Stripes of varying widths were painted in three shades of orange: Benjamin Moore latex flat 083, 089, and 007.

page 60, top and bottom: The base color is Benjamin Moore latex eggshell Linen White. The 12"-wide (30.5 cm) stripes were done in Benjamin Moore latex eggshell Decorators White latex mixed with Sunny's Goodtime Clear Glaze.

page 61, top left and right: The base color is Benjamin Moore oil semi-gloss Linen White. The pink and red stripes were done in Sign Painters' 1 SHOT Lettering Enamel. The entire piece was first lightly sanded and then aged with Old Masters Tinting Glaze mixed with raw umber artist's tube oil.

page 61, bottom: The cornice board base color is Benjamin Moore latex eggshell Linen White. The stripes and tractor were hand-painted in various artist's tube paints.

Horizontal stripes section:

page 62: The base color is a pale blue-gray, Benjamin Moore latex flat HC-150. The 12"-wide (30.5 cm) horizontal stripes were painted in medium chocolate brown, Benjamin Moore latex flat 992.

page 63: The base color is a yellow-orange, Benjamin Moore latex eggshell 310. Stripes of several widths were painted in brown, pink, green, and a very light tan (Benjamin Moore HC-69, 1326, 405, and 944).

pages 66 and 67: The base color is a warm tan, Benjamin Moore latex eggshell 1094. The 12"-wide (30.5 cm) horizontal stripes were washed on in Sunny's Goodtime Original Aging Glaze.

Plaid section:

page 68: The base color is a pale yellow, Benjamin Moore latex eggshell 338. The plaid was done in Sunny's Goodtime Summer Sun Glaze combination color (20 oz. Sunshine Daydream mixed with 4 oz. Original Aging Glaze).

page 69: The base color is a dark green, Benjamin Moore latex eggshell 567. The varying-width stripes were painted in Benjamin Moore beige (1066), pale blue (HC-144), and pale green (2028-50). The entire design was aged with Sunny's Original Aging Glaze.

page 74, top and bottom: The base color is a light blue, Benjamin Moore latex eggshell 813. The 12"-wide (30.5 cm) blue stripes were created by washing on with Sunny's Goodtime Marine Glaze.

page 75, top left and right: The base color of the dresser is Benjamin Moore latex flat Linen White. The plaid was created in green, pink, blue, and tan acrylic artist's paints. Sunny's Goodtime Metallic Gold was used on the knobs and edges. The entire piece was glazed with Sunny's Goodtime Original Aging Glaze.

page 75, bottom: The basecoat of the dresser is a chartreuse green, Benjamin Moore oil semi-gloss 404. The plaid was created in various Benjamin Moore oil flat colors: brown (1302), blue (823), yellow (350), green (567), peach (159), and black. The entire piece was aged with raw umber tube oil mixed with Old Masters Tinting Glaze applied with a rag.

Panels section:

pages 76 and 77: The base color is a warm yellow, Benjamin Moore latex eggshell 2020-50. The ¼" (6 mm) inner panel outline was done in rose, Benjamin Moore latex eggshell 1360, and the ½" (1.3 cm) outer outline was done in brown, Benjamin Moore latex eggshell HC-76.

page 80, top and bottom: The walls were first painted a light green, Benjamin Moore latex eggshell 491, and then the panels were painted light cream, Benjamin Moore latex eggshell Linen White. The panel outlining was done in Sunny's Goodtime Ruby Red Glaze and Gator Green Glaze.

page 81, top and bottom: The base color is a pale celadon green, Benjamin Moore latex eggshell 2028-60. The panels were washed with Sunny's Goodtime Bahama Blue Colour Wash. The second wash is Sunny's Goodtime Little Boy Blue Colour Wash. The narrow panel border was done in coral, Benjamin Moore latex eggshell 2009-30, with flowers stenciled over it in the original green.

page 82 top and bottom: The base color is a medium yellow (Farrow & Ball latex eggshell 218). The 2" (5 cm) panel outline was done in pink, Benjamin Moore latex eggshell 1360. The ¼" (6 mm) panel outline was done in brown, Benjamin Moore latex eggshell HC-76.

page 83: The base color is a pale blue-gray, Benjamin Moore latex eggshell 874. The panels were painted in Benjamin Moore latex eggshell White. The panels were outlined in a light gray, Benjamin Moore latex eggshell 871. The gold lines are Sunny's Goodtime Metallic Gold Stencil Paint.

Stoneblock section:

page 84: The base color is Benjamin Moore latex eggshell White. The stoneblocks were done in Sunny's Goodtime Original Aging Glaze, washed on with a rag.

page 85: The base color is Benjamin Moore latex eggshell White. The stoneblocks were done in Sunny's Goodtime Palm Beach Pink Colour Wash.

pages 90 and 91: The base color is Benjamin Moore latex eggshell White. The stoneblocks were done in Sunny's Goodtime Original Aging Glaze, washed on with a cheesecloth.

Diamond walls section:

page 92: The base color is a light gray, Benjamin Moore latex eggshell 975. The diamonds were painted in yellow-green and light green, Benjamin Moore latex eggshell 391 and 536.

page 93: The lavender base color is Benjamin Moore 2071-60. The diamonds are: orange-yellow, Benjamin

Moore 307; pink, Benjamin Moore 1327; gray, Benjamin Moore 1346; green, Benjamin Moore 405. The entire board was then aged in Sunny's Goodtime Take Me to Tuscany Aging Glaze. The brown dots are Benjamin Moore 992.

page 98, top and bottom: The base color is Benjamin Moore latex eggshell White. The diamonds were done in Sunny's Goodtime combination color (6 oz. Black Leather Glaze + 18 oz. French Gray Colour Wash), washed on with a cheesecloth. Sunny's Goodtime Metallic Gold Stencil Paint was sponged onto Sunny's Goodtime Dot Stencil.

page 99: The base color is a pale beige, Benjamin Moore latex eggshell 1066. Sunny's Goodtime Original Aging Glaze was applied with a rag to create the diamonds.

page 100 and 101: The diamonds were painted in Benjamin Moore Floor & Patio satin latex enamel Cliffside Gray and White (thinned down). The diamonds were outlined using the same paint in Platinum Gray.

page 106, top: The large diamonds were painted in Benjamin Moore Floor & Patio satin latex enamel White mixed with 50% water. The outline was done using the same paint in a light brown color (HC-76) and the small circles in the same paint in a lighter brown (HC-77).

page 106, bottom left and right: The basecoat is Benjamin Moore Floor & Patio satin latex enamel White. The diamonds were painted with the same paint in Platinum Gray and the diamond outline with 50% Platinum Gray + 50% Black.

page 107, top left and right: The diamonds were painted in Benjamin Moore Floor & Patio satin latex enamel Linen White and outlined in Brown. The floor was then glazed for depth.

page 107, bottom: The basecoat of the dresser is a chartreuse green, Benjamin Moore oil semi-gloss 404. The plaid was created in various Benjamin Moore oil flat colors: brown (1302), blue (823), yellow (350), green (567), peach (159), and black. The entire piece was aged with raw umber tube oil mixed with Old Masters Tinting Glaze applied with a rag.

Freehand section:

page 108: The freehand flower pattern was painted on with black acrylic tube paint.

page 109: The base color is a pale blue, Benjamin Moore latex eggshell HC-144. The freehand design was done in a light brown, Benjamin Moore latex eggshell HC-69. The entire piece was aged with Sunny's Goodtime Ocean Age Aging Glaze.

page 111: The rope was first painted with Benjamin Moore latex eggshell White; then the blue was added (Benjamin Moore latex eggshell 787). The base color of the wall is a green, Benjamin Moore latex eggshell 2028-60. Sunny's Goodtime Fern combination color (4 oz. Original Aging Glaze + 20 oz. Gator Green Glaze) was washed on with a rag below the freehand border.

page 112, top and bottom: The base color of the walls is a pale yellow, Benjamin Moore latex eggshell HC-5. Sunny's Goodtime Cantaloupe combination color (12 oz. Pumpkin Glaze + 12 oz. Sunshine Daydream Glaze) was washed on with a rag below the freehand border. The border was done in Sunny's Goodtime Fern Glaze, Ruby Red Glaze, and Pumpkin Glaze.

page 113, top: The base color of the walls is Benjamin Moore latex eggshell White. The stripes were done in a lime green, Benjamin Moore latex eggshell 403. The dots were done in Sunny's Goodtime Cantaloupe combination color (12 oz.

Pumpkin Glaze + 12 oz. Sunshine Daydream Glaze) and Sunny's Goodtime Bubblegum combination color (16 oz. Palm Beach Pink Colour Wash + 8 oz. Ruby Red Glaze).

page 113, lower left: The base color of the walls is Benjamin Moore latex eggshell White. Sunny's Goodtime Cappuccino Glaze, a light gray glaze, was washed on with a rag. The circles were painted in a medley of colors: yellow, purple, orange, green, and a reddish pink.

page 113, lower right: The vine was painted in a light green, Benjamin Moore latex eggshell 403, and the flower was painted in a medium rose, Benjamin Moore latex eggshell 1328. The doorknob was done in a light orange, Benjamin Moore latex eggshell 082.

page 114: The base color is a taupe, Benjamin Moore latex eggshell HC-91. Sunny's Goodtime French Gray Colour Wash and Sunny's Goodtime Take Me to Tuscany Glaze (terra-cotta color) were washed on with rags. The freehand scroll and Sunny's Goodtime Dot Stencil were both applied in Sunny's Goodtime French Gray Colour Wash.

page 115: The base color is Benjamin Moore latex eggshell Decorators White. Sunny's Goodtime Bubblegum Pink Glaze combination color (16 oz. Palm Beach Pink Colour Wash + 8 oz. Ruby Red Glaze) was washed on the walls with a rag. Sunny's Goodtime Dot Stencil was done in light lime green, Benjamin Moore latex eggshell 416. The freehand border was painted in a bright pink, Benjamin Moore latex eggshell 1346.

For more information on Benjamin Moore paints, contact them at: Benjamin Moore Paints, 51 Chestnut Ridge Road, Montvale, NJ 07645, or look on the Internet at http://www.benjaminmoore.com

Sunny's Colour Washes and Glazes

Colour Washes

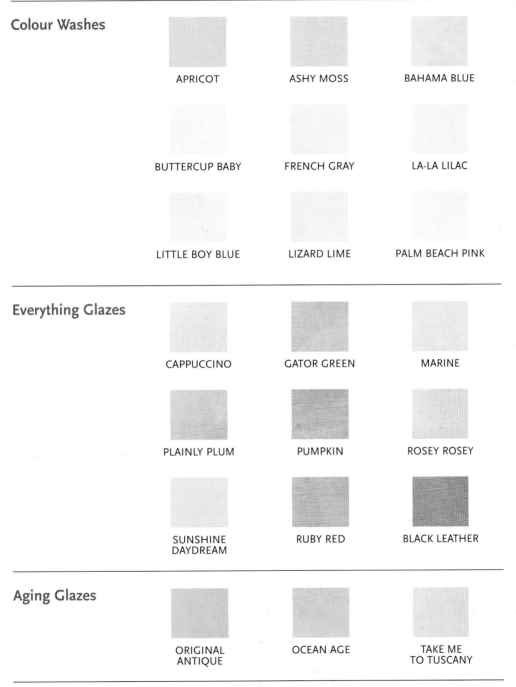

APRICOT   ASHY MOSS   BAHAMA BLUE

BUTTERCUP BABY   FRENCH GRAY   LA-LA LILAC

LITTLE BOY BLUE   LIZARD LIME   PALM BEACH PINK

Everything Glazes

CAPPUCCINO   GATOR GREEN   MARINE

PLAINLY PLUM   PUMPKIN   ROSEY ROSEY

SUNSHINE DAYDREAM   RUBY RED   BLACK LEATHER

Aging Glazes

ORIGINAL ANTIQUE   OCEAN AGE   TAKE ME TO TUSCANY

NOTE: Colors will vary depending on application and basecoat color.

Visit sunnysgoodtimepaint.com on the Internet for more information.

index

A

aging glaze, 46-53: on walls and furniture, 43, 50, 51, 52, 53; curtain rods, 52; instructions, 48-49; and stencil, 46-49; swatch chart, 123; and tube oils, 49

B

basecoat, 14, 21, 26

bathroom: brown striped, 62–65; with colored circles, 113; green stenciled, 35; with diamond walls, 98; with freehand flowers, 108–110

bedroom: beige glazed, 44; blue check, 74; with canopy, 7, 114–115; green with scallops, 9, 28; with rope border, 111; with wavy stripes, 113

brushes, 17

C

canopy (freehand), 7, 114–115

ceilings: for dark house, 10; raising visually, 6, 12; half-strength, 9

chair, 50

chalk, 17

chalkboard paint, 12

child's room: blue check, 74; diamond walls, 11, 99; with green scalloped border, 9, 28; with rope border, 111; stoneblock in, 10, 90–91; tonal stripes in, 66–67

choosing a project, 20

color: darker when dry, 17, 26; and mood, 5, 6; and harmony, 10; testing, 17, 26; 3-color rule, 8

colorwash, 24–29: basecoat for, 26; choosing, 25; for diamonds, 97; and glaze, 25, 114–115; green room, 28; instructions, 24–26; and panels, 79; pink dining room, 29; pool house, 28; swatch chart, 123

cornice, 61

D

diamond floor, 100–107

diamond walls, 92–99: in bathroom, 98; in child's room, 11, 99; instructions, 92–97; size of, 93; on test board, 93; to unify space, 101

dining room: pale pink, 29; with panels, 80, 81, 83; stenciled, 30–34, 46–49; with thin panel outlines, 13, 80; yellow glazed, 42

dresser, 61, 75, 107

drying time: of basecoat, 21; of glaze, 38

E

enlarging room visually, 6

entrance hall, 36, 45, 68, 84, 106

F

finishes, 14

floors, 20, 22, 102, 100–107

flower and vine border, 112

freehand: 108–115; bathroom, 108–110; canopy, 7, 114–115; circles and doorknobs, 113; borders, 111, 112; instructions, 108–110; vine pattern, 109; wavy stripes, 113

furniture (painted): cabinet, 5, 51, 53, 59; chair, 50; chest or dresser, 2, 61, 75, 107; shelves, 52; tables, 53

G

glaze, 36–45: and basecoat, 39; in beige bedroom, 44; brushstrokes in, 73; compared to colorwash, 37; for diamonds, 97; drying time of, 38; effect of, 37, 38; instructions, 38–39; with oil-based paint, 39, 49; in pink entry hall, 45; in pink sitting room, 22, 40, 43; rags for, 39; for stoneblock, 88–89; swatch chart for, 123; in tan den, 41. See also Aging glaze.

glossary of paint terms, 116–117

H

half-strength paint, 9

horizontal stripes, 8, 62–67: brown, 62–65; instructions, 62–65; tonal, 66–67

I

irregularly shaped rooms, 55

K

kitchen cabinets and walls, 9, 59, 92–99

L

latex paint, 15, 20, 39, 49

level (tool), 17, 19, 73, 86

living room: glazed, 43; green, 24; light orange, 27; with tonal stripes, 60; with panels, 4, 8, 10, 13, 76–83

N

nail polish remover (to test paint), 20

O

oil-based paint, 15, 20, 21, 39, 49

oil paint (tube), for aging glaze, 49

P

paint: coats, 14; drying times, 21, 38; glazes for, 39, 49, 123; latex, 15, 20, 39, 49; primer, 14, 19, 21; swatch chart of glazes and washes, 123; terms, 14–15, 116–117; testing if oil- or latex based, 20

painter's tape, 16

panels, 76–83: instructions, 76–79; with double lines, 4, 8, 10, 13, 76–83; with stenciled border, 81

plaid, 68–75: in child's blue bedroom, 74; on dresser, 75; instructions, 68–73; sample board, 69

pool house, 21, 28

preparation for painting, 21

primer, 14, 19, 21

S

scuff marks, 21

sitting room: green striped, 54–61; pink, with diamond floor, 22, 40; with pinstripes, 6, 59

small space, 101

stencil, 30–35: cutting your own, 33; damask pattern, 30–35; with diamonds, 93, 98, 103; on green bathroom, 35; instructions, 30–33; palm, 31; scale of, 31–32; stenciled border of panel, 11, 81; with vertical stripes, 57

stoneblock, 84–91: in child's room, 10, 90–91; glazing, 88; instructions, 84–89

stripes. See vertical stripes and horizontal stripes.

Sunny's 3-color rule, 8

supplies, 16–19, 26

swatch chart of colorwashes and glazes, 123

T

tonal colors, 58, 60, 66–67, 74, 97

tools and supplies, 16–19, 26

top coats, 14–15

trim color, 10

U

unifying rooms with color, 10, 11, 101

V

Venetian plaster entry hall, 45

vertical stripes, 54–61: on cornice, 61; on dresser, 61; on entrance hall, 58; green, 54–61; instructions, 54–57; in irregular rooms, 55; in kitchen cabinet, 9, 59; pinstripes, 59; stencil with, 57; tonal, 58, 60; wavy, 113; width of, 57

vine pattern (freehand), 109

W

wooden floor, 20, 22